INLAND CRUISERS

Care and Maintenance

Nick Billingham

The Crowood Press

First published in 1995 by
The Crowood Press Ltd
Ramsbury, Marlborough
Wiltshire SN8 2HR

British Library Cataloguing-in-Publication Data
A catalogue record for this book is available from the British
Library.

ISBN 1 85223 908 5

Picture Credits
All photographs by Nick Billingham
All line-drawings by Bob Constant

Dedication

This book is dedicated to my daughter Victoria

Typeset by Phoenix Typesetting, Ilkley, West Yorkshire
Printed and bound in Great Britain by The Bath Press

Contents

Acknowledgements

I would like to thank the following businesses and individuals for their invaluable help in the preparation of this book; British Waterways Board, particularly for their help with the Boat Safety Scheme, Swallow Cruisers of Hockley Heath, Womborne Canal Services, Stratford Marina, Welford Boat Station, and all the many boat owners who have allowed their boats to be photographed.

NOTE: This book is intended for guidance only. Whenever you are carrying out any work on a boat it is imperative that it be done with due regard to all the safety procedures required. Any alterations or additions to a boat must meet with the boat or system manufacturers' specifications, and all work must comply with the relevant Codes of Practice.

Preface

Cabin cruisers are an inexpensive way to explore the inland waterways. They have a shallow draught, allowing them to travel along canals and rivers inaccessible to larger boats, and they have engines and fittings that are easy to service and repair. They can be winched up on trailers and driven overland in a few hours to be launched on waterways that would take weeks to cruise to, or are even completely inaccessible to boats on the main waterways. Cruisers are versatile and fun.

Every boat, regardless of its size or value, needs to be maintained in a sensible way. Small or large, you don't want the motor to fail when you are by a weir; the wiring must be inspected every so often to prevent any little fault becoming a potential fire risk; and there are new rules governing the installation of outboard motors and gas supplies with which every boat owner needs to be familiar.

This book is intended to be a guide to the maintenance of cruisers; it introduces a schedule of work so that all the major systems on board will receive due attention, and so that potential faults may be identified before they occur. Fault prevention is the key to successful cruising, and a well maintained boat suffers fewer breakdowns than one that is left until something goes wrong. Boating enjoys a very low rate of accidents, and good care of the boat is a key element in this record.

Cruisers are straightforward to work on. Even the most complicated of boats can be divided into a series of separate systems, each with its own requirements. As inland cruising has become more popular, boats have become increasingly well equipped. Gone are the days of a canoe and tent; a modern cruiser can carry most of the comforts of home, albeit in a somewhat more compact space.

However, as boats have become more complicated, so has the paperwork, and the British Waterways Safety Standards that were introduced in 1990 seemed particularly onerous on cruiser owners; the raft of regulations covering petrol and gas installations, and hull integrity and inspection led many boat owners to wonder whether they weren't the victim of a plot designed to clear cruisers off the waterways for good. Luckily common sense has prevailed, and the revised Boat Safety Scheme is more flexible and straightforward to implement. The scheme does nevertheless still contain a great number of regulations and standards, and so Chapter Seven is dedicated to a detailed examination of all the relevant clauses and how they can be put into practice. Cruisers are, inevitably, prone to problems because they use petrol and gas, both of which are capable of causing fires and explosions if handled carelessly, and need to be treated with respect.

A well maintained boat is the key to a world of exploration of the waterways, relaxing holidays and a gentle pace of life.

Introduction

A boat is a machine, and thus needs to be adequately maintained to be able to fulfil its function properly. In fact a boat is a whole host of smaller machines and systems working together to make up a vehicle which will provide you and your family with wonderful holidays . . . as long as they all work the way they are supposed to. Unfortunately it only takes one small component to fail and the boat can be left without power or water, heat or light, and a well earned break on the waterways can be ruined. By looking after each part and system according to its own needs, the chances of catastrophic breakdowns are reduced. The resulting confidence in your boat will enhance the pleasure of a cruise and encourage you to tackle even more adventurous journeys.

Looking after a boat is not a particularly difficult task. To the novice it all looks complicated and daunting, but really a boat is composed of a set of simple machines and systems, each one working according to the fundamental laws of physics. Once those laws are understood, locating faults becomes a simple process of elimination. It's very easy to think, especially with some older outboard motors, that a machine has a particular grudge against you, and won't work out of sheer spite; but really if the conditions are right for it to work, then it must work. This is the nature of physics.

Luckily for boaters the principles for keeping a boat afloat and working are the basic ones that we learnt at school, and probably promptly forgot after the exams. But once the cobwebs are brushed off, they are as relevant to boats today as they ever were. Boats are simple enough; no fiendish calculations are needed, simply an awareness of what makes each system tick, and a schedule for the maintenance of each one will provide the boater with a structure on which to base the ongoing care of the craft.

Boats need a regular amount of work to keep them at their optimum, which means that 'little and often' is the best policy; 'lots once in a blue moon' nearly always means that the boat is rarely in prime condition at the start of a cruise. Who knows when the opportunity for a quick weekend away will arise? One of the real pleasures of boating is when an unexpected day off work and a fine weather forecast for the weekend means that you can grab a few belongings, nip down to the boat and potter off up the river. If the boat is moored up, clean and working, ready to go, then a brilliant break is in store. But if care of the boat has been postponed for the last year or so, then there is every chance that most of the weekend will be spent trying to get it started or repaired, and by the time the motor is going and the problems solved it will be time to think about going home, and the idyllic weekend away will have been wasted.

The idea behind this book is to break down the various elements that comprise a boat into their separate systems, and to examine each of these for its own particular maintenance requirements. A trailer, for instance, has very different needs to a gas cooker, but both are capable of killing you if they fail badly, so need to be looked after properly.

Boating is a fairly safe hobby, but there are

potential hazards on board and it is the owner's duty to ensure that his friends and family are not exposed to danger. Each year a handful of fatal accidents occurs, some of which have been caused by a lack of understanding of potential risks. Petrol vapour is usually the prime culprit; it is heavy and sinks to the bottom of the bilges, and it can and does ignite and explode should a spark come into contact with it, with horrific consequences. Gas behaves in the same way, and both fuels need to be treated with respect. Other accidents are caused because those in charge fail to appreciate the sheer momentum of a boat, or simply by bad driving. A boat that is badly maintained can become a killer, so a clear plan of maintenance is essential for the longevity of the crew as well as the craft.

Although virtually everything on board a boat can be serviced and repaired by a competent amateur mechanic, modern rules and regulations have taken some fields of expertise into the world of the professional. Gas systems in particular are no longer the province of the DIY boater. There have been so many accidents caused by LPG installations that there are now dozens of rules and regulations that have to be taken into account. In practice this has meant that gas systems on boats have to be fitted and inspected by registered and approved fitters, and the new Boat Safety Scheme lends weight to this. For the boat owner this means an additional expense that he may feel is unwarranted; nevertheless, the number of explosions and deaths from carbon monoxide poisoning has dropped as a result, so the expense is worthwhile.

It may not be too far into the future that petrol engines are covered by similar legislation, for just the same reasons. It is therefore important to remember the hazards when working with petrol, and to be extra vigilant. The Boat Safety Scheme has plenty to say about petrol installations, all designed to reduce the number of accidents. It may be a lot of paperwork interfering with the important business of getting out onto the water; but safety is a vital issue for all of us, and it would be irresponsible not to take it seriously.

But enough of these dire warnings of explosions and sinkings: when all is said and done, boating is one of the safest pastimes, and it must be the very best way to see the heart of a beautiful country. There can be few better pleasures in life than sitting on deck watching a kingfisher diving from a willow into the sun-dappled waters of a gentle river. So let's make sure the boat will get us there ...

— 1 —

Hull and Superstructure

The Principles of Boat Design

The basic structure of a cruiser consists of a hull and superstructure. The hull is designed to keep the river out and to allow the boat to travel through the water in the most efficient manner for the use it is designed for. Thus a slow-going canal cruiser will have a displacement type hull, whereas a faster river or estuary boat will probably have a planing hull. The difference in their performance is very noticeable when they are going at speeds other than their design intended them to; thus a planing hull with its V-shaped bottom will create very little wash once it is up on its plane and whizzing along at twenty or thirty miles an hour, but problems occur when it can't do this: it isn't designed to part the water gently, and so it shoves a massive wash to the side. Displacement hulls, on the other hand, work wonderfully at low speeds producing very little wash, but can be truly terrifying if you try to get them up to thirty miles an hour. It is therefore worth bearing

Hull profiles.

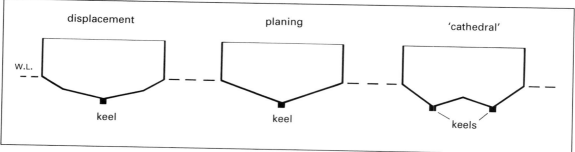

Hull cross-sections.

this difference in mind when you look at a boat with a view to buying it: an estuary boat may well look very smart, but if it is incapable of travelling at slow speed without washing the fishermen off the banks then it is not going to be a good buy if your intention is to cruise inland rivers and canals.

The design of the hull also affects the stability of a boat. A boat will always rock from side to side as you get on and off, but the amount it rocks depends on several factors, all of which have a bearing on the use to which it will be put. As a general rule the heavier a boat is, the more stable it will be. The weight will then affect the draught of a boat. Boat designers have to tread a delicate path between having a boat that is very stable but with a deep draught, or with less draught and therefore less stability. Moreover on inland waterways a deep draught is a draw-back, and anything over three feet is asking for constant trouble. To maintain an adequate weight with a low draught the boat's hull needs to be made fairly flat-bottomed, in a shallow vee, or with twin keels.

Inland boats also have a height restriction: bridges. A boat that has more than 7 ft (2.1m) of air draught (above the waterline) may find that it has trouble on some canals, and as a result most cruisers are designed with a fold-ing cockpit cover. The height above water added to the draught then determines the available headroom in the boat. The designer

is probably in tears at this point, because the boat simply doesn't weigh enough to displace sufficient water to provide adequate head-room inside.

The superstructure is the part above the gunwales; it keeps the rain off and supports masts, handrails and suchlike. The higher the structure, the more it will raise the centre of gravity of the craft and adversely affect the stability. It will also catch the wind and make the boat difficult to handle in rough weather, and will see you bouncing off every lock wall and bridge that you meet. On the other hand, if it is too low you will spend all your holi-days bent over nearly double.

All in all, designing the ideal cruiser is not an easy task, but it is worth knowing the basics so that when looking at a new boat you will be able to judge its intended function from its appearance.

Hull Construction

Cruisers are generally made from GRP or glass-reinforced plastic (fibreglass, to you and me), a versatile and sturdy material requiring very little maintenance. There are also plenty of wooden cruisers still about, and with care and attention they should last just as long as the plastic boats. Finally some cruisers are made of steel, but not that many as steel doesn't bend easily to the compound curves needed for the hull shapes.

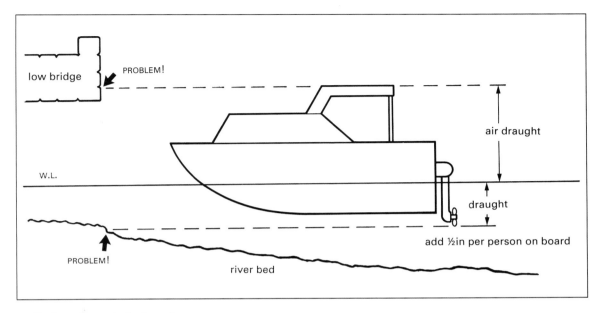

Hull: draught and air draught.

Fibreglass Boats

Fibreglass is by far the most common material for cruiser hulls, and with good reason: first a well made GRP hull should last virtually indefinitely. It is resistant to nearly all the common corrosive elements it is likely to encounter, such as salt- or fresh water, petrol, diesel and battery acid. It does suffer from exposure to ultra-violet light over time, and after a decade or two may well require an additional surface of paint to perk up its appearance; but if it is well made initially, it should remain in good condition.

To keep the boat looking in mint condition it is best to keep it well polished with a proprietary fibreglass polish; this has the effect of keeping the water and sunlight a few millionths of an inch away from the plastic, which might not be far, but is enough to slow down the ageing process considerably. It also keeps the boat looking at its smartest all year round. Two or three polishes a year are about the least you can get away with, once a month

in the summer is best – and once a week is overdoing it because you will want some time actually to use the boat!

The top half of the boat, or superstructure, is inevitably a lot more cluttered than the hull. The boat is most likely to have been made in two halves, the top and bottom; these are subsequently stuck together at the gunwales behind the rubbing strake. The top half needs to be just as strong as the bottom, particularly as it has a lot more holes cut in it which reduce its overall strength, and the roof has to take the weight of crew members clambering on and off in locks. Moreover every hole in it represents a route for rainwater to enter the cabin area.

Maintenance and Repair of Fibreglass Boats

Osmosis
The biggest worry for boat owners is the dreaded osmosis, often called 'boat pox' because of the appearance of the surface

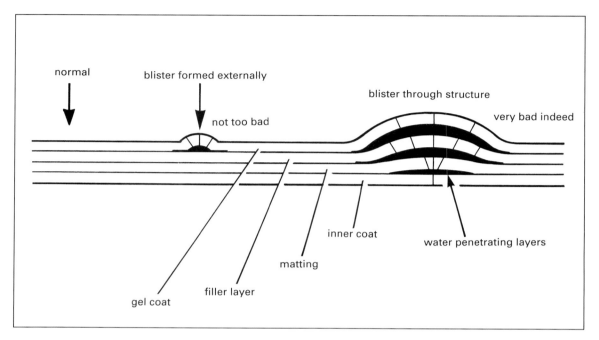

GRP structure and osmosis.

damage. In fact it isn't too great a disaster if your cruiser starts to suffer from it, but it is worth understanding the processes at work in order to prevent it occurring. Osmosis can be the result of poor manufacture, and it can be the result of misuse.

The fibreglass structure is a laminate of several layers of hardened plastic on top of and incorporating a glass-fibre matting; the more layers the stronger it is, and the more expensive. Each layer has to be made of an exact mixture of resin and catalyst, cured at a precise temperature. The technology of the plastic might seem simple for a quick repair or for patching up a bit of rust as on a car, but when making a boat the conditions must be perfect. Poor construction can result in a bad bond between the layers, and in small cracks in the outer gel coat, and the causes of future problems are then built into the boat. Thus once the boat has been in the water for a year or two the water will have seeped into the

laminated structure through these cracks, and when it freezes it will expand and rupture the surface. In salt-water conditions, salt is drawn into the fabric, left there as the water dries and gradually builds up, again expanding and cracking the material. When osmosis occurs because of this, the resulting damage can be extensive and may look horrendous.

Osmosis can be induced by abuse and ageing. The normal structure of fibreglass is to have only one side protected by a gel coat. Look on the inside of the hull and the glass matting will be seen embedded in the plastic. This internal surface has a much weaker water resistance, and it is quite easy for damp to seep into the fibres, and from there into the laminate.

It is wise always to keep the bilges dry. Cracks also provide a route for water to enter the laminate, so it is vital to repair any serious cracks before damage occurs. Any boat will develop a myriad tiny little cracks from the

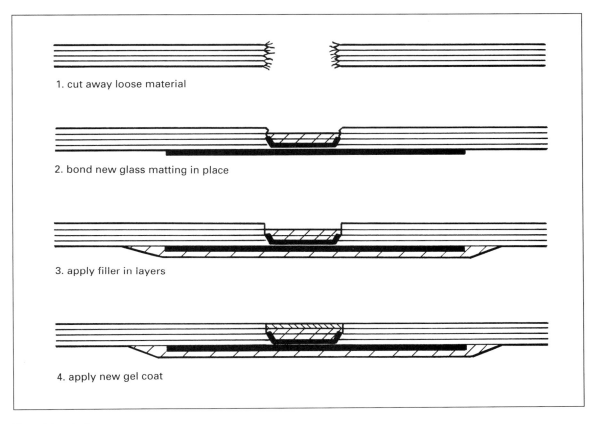

1. cut away loose material

2. bond new glass matting in place

3. apply filler in layers

4. apply new gel coat

Repairing holes.

everyday rough and tumble of boating; if these are only confined to the outer layer of the gel coat they do not represent a hazard, but cracks that extend through to the laminate layers need to be repaired promptly.

Because inland cruisers are not exposed to salt water, they do not disintegrate that rapidly when they suffer from this sort of damage. Salt-water boaters, however, have a very serious problem with osmosis, and yachts can often be seen with vast swathes of their outer skin peeling off. Nevertheless, depending on the severity of the damage the cure is not usually too drastic. If a boat is badly affected it is normally best to get a professional repair job; there are several companies who will not only repair osmosis damage, but will also offer a long-term guarantee on the work.

The normal damage in this category is a speckling of the surface, particularly along the waterline. When the hull starts looking as though it is developing blackheads, it is time to act because in a few years' time these could start looking like a bad case of smallpox and the problem will be much more difficult to solve. Whilst the material structure is still sound it is simple enough to dry the boat out, sand down the surface and paint the surface with a good quality, two-part epoxy resin paint. This will effectively seal the gel coat and restore the waterproof integrity of the material. It will also make the boat look like new if it is done properly.

Cracks and dents like this can be repaired.

In fact osmosis is comparatively rare on inland boats, so you shouldn't need to worry about it. However, it is always worth pulling the boat out of the water once a year and examining the hull closely to be sure that a small problem doesn't mature into a major crisis.

Specific Repairs

Collision damage is a somewhat more dramatic reason for working on the fibreglass. It is all too easy to slam the boat into a wharf, crunch over a bicycle or even bounce into another boat. Fibreglass is an immensely strong material with plenty of spring in it, but there are occasions when it can be cracked or holed.

Where a **hole or crack** has to be repaired, the most important thing is to ascertain the extent of the damage. With a sharp puncture, the hole is likely to be a clean one with little surrounding cracking; by contrast, a heavy knock against a bridge may not even hole the boat but it will leave a web of cracks radiating away from the impact point for several feet in every direction. In this instance the cabin lining must be removed so that the damaged area can be fully inspected inside as well as out.

The area damaged will need to be repaired in two ways. First, the structural integrity must be re-established by bonding a new layer of glass-fibre mat over the cracks and the back of the hole on the inside. Fresh fibreglass resin will stick to the old material very well, as long as there are no contaminants;

thus paint, wax, grease and dirt must be cleaned off the old material. The procedure is to key up the area with a thin coat of resin, bond a layer of matting on, allow that to cure, brush on another layer of resin and another layer of matting, and so on. Three layers will suffice for non load-bearing parts of the boat, and five or more for areas that will take stress. If the cracks cross corners, sharp curves or highly stressed parts of the hull such as the bows or transom, then it would be wise to seek the advice of a professional.

The second part of the repair is to ensure that the hull surface is returned to its original condition. The cracks will need to be grooved out and a fresh filler inserted.

Where a **piece of material is missing**, the smooth hull line can be restored by using sev-eral layers to build up the new filler to the old surface level. It is also possible to buy dyes to colour the new filler to a shade similar to the original; this can be a tricky business, but it is perfectly possible to repair the damage so well that it is invisible.

A part of the hull that often needs repair is the **area surrounding the deck fittings.** Cleats are often pulled heavily, and over time their bolts work loose and erode the fibreglass around them; it is therefore worth checking that this isn't happening whilst the annual hull examination is being done. The holes can easily be firmed up with some fresh plastic, and if necessary a wooden or steel pad can be bonded into place to spread the load.

Fibreglass resin is a demanding material to work with, because once the resin and

Make sure that deck fittings are securely fitted.

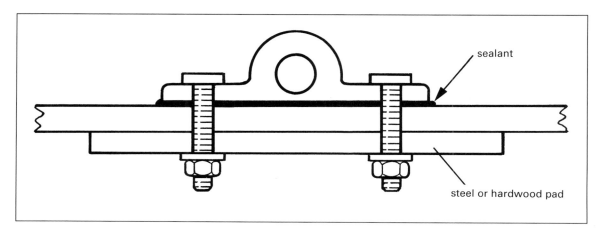

Strengthening deck fittings.

catalyst are mixed thoroughly, it will set in a matter of minutes. How quickly is dependent on the temperature: below about 5° it will take too long to form a good bond, and above 30° it will be too quick. The resin must be mixed in clean and dry conditions; a high humidity in the air will contaminate the mix, as will high dust levels. The resin will bond to almost anything, fingers, eyes, clothes and especially itself, so take care. Read the instructions and follow them scrupulously.

Structural Bearers

Every fibreglass boat contains load-bearing spars within the GRP moulding. These are normally pieces of timber incorporated into the bows, transom, gunwales and roof which provide extra rigidity and strength, allowing the forces from the outboard motor to be transmitted throughout the hull. They also help to ensure that if a crew member jumps from the lock side down onto the roof, he doesn't go right through it! These struts need to be inspected every two years to ensure that the wood inside them is not exposed to damp; if it is, it can rot right away, leaving a hole and a weak spot in the hull. If this happens new timbers can be glassed into place to replace them, but professional advice should be

sought to make sure that the original strength is restored.

Painting Fibreglass Boats

As already mentioned, fibreglass is resistant to most everyday chemicals such as solvents and fuels, and unfortunately this also includes paints. So the basic problem when painting a GRP boat is, how to make the paint stick to a surface that doesn't want to take it? Moreover the process has to be done properly because a boat with paint peeling off it looks ghastly.

Preparing the Surface

Simply preparing the surface for painting is a laborious task, but it is the most crucial part of the entire process because it is the basis for all subsequent work: if the boat's surface isn't utterly clean, all paints will flake off. Nevertheless, no matter how old and battered a boat, a new coat of paint will make it look almost as new. The main problem is that there are waxes, oils and other contaminants on the hull surface which must be removed. A good scrub with thinners will remove the worst of these, the oils, waxes and narrow boat black, and this then needs to be followed with a detergent wash to remove all the thinners (there are special detergents available from paint manufacturers for this purpose).

At this stage most of the grubbiness of the boat may have disappeared, and it may not really need a coat of paint at all, just a good wax polish. It is surprising how quickly a surface patina of dirt can build up, and how much better a boat looks for a really thorough clean; and if it doesn't need painting, then don't do it. The process is irreversible and a paint surface will never quite match that of the original.

Choosing the Paint

If the boat definitely does need a coat of paint, then it is time to decide which paint to use. There are two main types suitable for GRP: epoxy-based paints that virtually mimic the gel coat, and ordinary marine-grade paints. Cheap paints are worse than useless, because not only will they waste the time you spend in putting them on, but when they peel off they will seriously detract from the value of the boat.

Paint-makers generally provide full information sheets so that users can get the best results. Each paint system has its own routine of etch primers, undercoats, fillers and gloss coats, and if these are followed to the letter you can't go wrong . . . but remember, in the very first instance an absolutely clean surface is the key element. I cannot stress this too much, before you start, the surface to be painted must be utterly and completely clean; if it isn't, all the fancy paint in the world won't help.

Paint can be applied by brush roller or heavy duty spray gun. Good quality brushes provide the best finish; rollers do the job much faster but with a less than smooth finish. A good compromise is to have one person applying the paint with a roller, and a second laying off the paint to a fine finish with a high quality brush. There is quite an art to getting a really good finish. Practice

makes perfect, of course, as does always cleaning the brushes well. An old, well cared for brush is easier to use than a new one since the traces of old paint bind the bristles together; a brand new brush loses bristles into the paint film for some time. The instructions concerning drying times, particularly for undercoats, are very important: if a coat is applied over a layer of paint that isn't properly dry, the solvent trapped inside will bubble up in warm weather and cause peeling later; and if a coat is left to dry for too long it will become too hard before the succeeding coat is applied, and will have lost a degree of its adhesive properties – it will not bond as well to the new paint. If this happens, a rub down with fine sandpaper will key up the surface again.

The painting process allows for filler to be used on all those little scratches. On an old boat this can take ages; finding each crack and filling it with resin filler, then sanding it smooth seems to go on for ever. A batch of filler is only good for five minutes or so, so it pays to make up small quantities; but remember, it is much more difficult to get the proportions of resin and catalyst exactly right with small amounts, so take extra care.

The weather can exert a powerful influence on the drying times of paints. Cruisers are usually small enough to be towed into a barn or large garage where the temperature is more even than it is outside, and to some extent more controllable as well. If you can possibly arrange this, it will make the whole painting process very much easier.

Anti-fouling Paints

Beneath the waterline the hull needs to be treated with an anti-fouling paint. This treatment will have been first applied when the boat was brand new, and if it is regularly renewed there should never be any problems with the bond between the paint and the boat.

Anti-fouling paints for inland use do not contain the lethal cocktail of chemicals as in those used by sea-going craft. In fact even ocean-going boats are having to stop using toxic anti-fouling paints. Water weeds will grow on just about any surface in the water, and the original purpose of the paint was to render the surface of the hull so toxic that nothing could survive contact with it. Eventually this led to nothing surviving contact with the water near it, and a pollution problem arose. Modern anti-foulings use different ways to meet the same end. The paints tend to have a difficult surface for plants to adhere to, and can erode away, thus loosening the plants' grip.

By far the easiest way to use anti-foulings is to repaint with them once a year. Haul the boat up on a trailer, scrub off the old paint down to a reasonable surface, allow to dry, and then paint on another coat. The best times and conditions vary between paint-makers, so check the instructions on the tin. Anti-fouling paints must *never* be burnt off a boat; always scrub and sand them off, and always use a face mask while doing it. New anti-foulings are not too bad, but a lungful of dust from an old type of anti-fouling will be poisonous. Even if the boat is so old that there is no trace of the old anti-fouling, or if none has ever been applied, be careful nevertheless to take the same precautions when sanding the surface down, just in case there *are* residual traces there, that you can't see.

Summary

An absolutely clean surface is vital to ensure good paint adhesion. The paint-makers' instructions are not written to pass the time of day, they are there to ensure that the very best results are obtained from their product, so follow them scrupulously. All paints, and especially anti-foulings, contain irritant or toxic properties; this must be borne in mind when dealing with them.

Wooden Cruisers

A cabin cruiser made from wood is becoming an increasingly rare sight. This is a shame, really, because wood is a very amenable material to work with; it is environmentally friendly, taking carbon dioxide out of the air as it grows, and if it is treated with care will last forty or fifty years. On the other hand we may yet see more cruisers made from wood, as the cost of GRP rises because of the cost of the oil products it needs for its manufacture.

Twenty years ago there were plenty of wooden boats on the waterways, and a good few of those were hand-built by their owners. In the early days of inland boating, ships' lifeboats were a common sight too, though sadly these have become a rarity. They may have been cheap and cheerful, but they were a means whereby people could get onto the water for a modest amount of cash, and the more people there are boating, the brighter the future for our canals.

Wooden boats are more demanding. The structure for a cabin cruiser is usually a marine-grade plywood shell screwed to a hardwood frame consisting of keel, chines, ribs and transom. There are carvel and clinker-built boats too, comprised of planks of solid wood fixed to the boat's ribs and keel; however, these are usually found on estuary and sea-going boats.

A wooden hull does have the inherent drawback that it can rot. Marine-grade ply is very strong and resilient, but if maintenance is neglected the forces of nature will get to work, with devastating effect: a natural recycling scheme to turn the boat back into plant food and thus back into new trees!

Maintenance and Repair of Wooden Boats

The paintwork on a wooden boat is the most important barrier to the rotting process. It prevents water and air getting into the

Wooden boats are more demanding . . .

. . . or they disintegrate quickly.

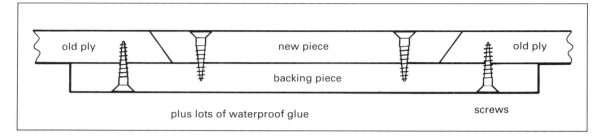

Wooden hull repairs.

cellular structure of the timber, and this denies fungi and bacteria the basics of survival; effectively it pickles the timbers. Lavish treatments with wood preservative also help. Even the bilges and every surface behind the cabin lining will need to be treated and painted; though fortunately wood is much easier to paint that GRP, so the task isn't nearly so exacting. The paint for a wooden boat needs to be able to flex with the wood: wood swells in the cool winter weather and shrinks in the summer, and the paint has to be able to accommodate this. Paint companies have developed some very effective wood paints for boats.

So a wooden hull is likely to suffer from rot in the places where water can enter the fabric of the wood: this is usually on parts of the superstructure where the water lies in puddles, rather than running off the boat quickly after rain. Therefore check that all the deck draining gulleys are working. Any puddle left on deck after a shower needs to be investigated and the reasons for it resolved. Deck areas prone to scuffing from shoes will need an extra layer of hard non-slip paint to give added protection. (It is easy to make a small amount of non-slip paint the same colour as the rest of the boat: take a small tub of the ordinary paint, and stir in a handful of dry, sharp sand; then paint this in the pattern to suit the non-slip area and let it dry thoroughly. It takes longer to dry than a coat of normal paint.)

The hull itself is prone to water damage where the paintwork is damaged regularly. The chines and corners of the transom are the parts of the boat most readily scraped against wharves and locks; extra hardwood rubbing strakes and plenty of bouncy fenders will reduce this damage, but will not mean you avoid it altogether. Also, the transom itself

Wooden boat repairs: cut away all broken wood . . .

takes all the thrust of the outboard motor, and if the boat is accelerated and stopped hard the flexing that this thrust produces will crack the paint; this thrust can be very marked during an emergency stop, or if the engine is run aground. It is therefore important to check this area for structural weakness very carefully each year.

Holes

Repairing holes in a plywood hull is simple enough. First, the extent of the damage needs to be assessed and the broken wood removed. Then a repair patch of the same dimensions should be cut and inserted into the hole, and fastened with a larger piece screwed and bolted behind it. Plenty of waterproof adhesive will ensure that the patch is as strong as the original timber. If a rib is broken, a new section can be dovetailed in place or additional timber bolted alongside. However, if the boat's keel is broken the damage may be so serious that repair is simply not cost-effective. Old wooden cruisers that have reached this stage can be used as interesting features in a flower garden, or as a truly splendid centrepiece to a bonfire night party.

Idiosyncrasies

Wooden boats have quirks of their own. You can repaint the hull and check that the whole thing appears utterly watertight on dry land, but as soon as it goes in the water it will almost certainly leak like a sieve for a day or two: no matter how hard you try to exclude the water, the joints on a wooden hull are never truly watertight until the wood is the correct humidity and the water pressure is compressing them. Also, wooden boats need to have all their fittings attached with brass

. . . and use generous patches.

or stainless steel screws or bolts. Ordinary steel will corrode away before your eyes because of the tannic acid contained in wood, and especially in oak; this substance will rot the steel at an alarming rate.

Engine Alignment

An inboard engine on a wooden boat can set up excessive vibration of the hull and shake it to bits if it is not correctly aligned. It is therefore always important to check the engine alignment each year.

Steel Boats

Steel might not rot or suffer from osmosis, and it is incredibly strong, but it rusts at an alarming rate. Even with sacrificial anodes welded or bolted to the hull below the water-line, there are still plenty of corners in the superstructure where rust can get a hold. How many and how big the anodes should be depends on the size of the boat; 5kg (11lb) per 30ft (9m) length is a rough estimate, but this will vary according to the make of anode. The anodes for fresh water are normally made of magnesium, but which metal is best will depend on the type of water you moor up in; different rivers and canals have markedly different characteristics when it comes to eating steel boats.

As with any boat, paint is the key to stopping corrosion. Note that steel, like wood, also has a high thermal expansion rate, and at least five coats of paint will be needed to get a film thick enough to flex with it; a paint surface less than 125 microns thick will crack, and let the water in.

On the whole, steel is so tough that repairs to the hull are not needed. Dents can be banged out with a hammer if the steel is thin enough, though use ear protectors to safeguard your hearing!

Cruiser Fittings

Windows

Cruiser windows are usually aluminium frames fitted with toughened glass; there are several companies which specialize in their manufacture and can make a replacement window if needed. The frames are fixed to the boat by a variety of methods: best of all are stainless steel nuts and bolts; the worst are ordinary pop-rivets, and in between are self-tapping screws and gas tight rivets.

Boats with steel nuts and bolts will probably never need attention unless the window is broken by accident. Self-tapping screws will eventually wear out the fibreglass that they are screwed into, and the window will loosen and leak, and will need to be removed

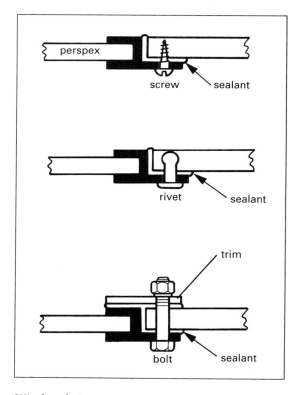

Window fixings.

Windows need to be watertight.

and cleaned. The holes will then be too big to accept new screws, and each screw hole will need to be filled up a bit with new resin before the window can be replaced with a fresh bead of silicon sealant. Gas-tight rivets behave in much the same way as self-tapping screws.

Pop-rivets are simply a confounded nuisance. They leak through the centre hole from the very moment they are installed, they are difficult to remove, and a waste of time to replace. If you need to reseal a window held in by pop-rivets, the best procedure is to drill off the heads and push out the centres to release the frame, check the hole diameter, and then buy some proper stainless steel nuts and bolts which will do the job properly. Old Dawncrafts are notorious for these pop-rivets, and their plastic front windscreens need replacing every eight or nine years

because of cracking and fading. They are marvellous boats, except for this one feature.

Hand Rails

Grab rails are important to keep the crew on board. Stainless steel rails securely bolted to the roof are best of all; wooden rails can look very appealing but suffer from wood rot. They need to be inspected regularly, and this can be done by giving them an extra hard tug; if they come off in your hand, it is time to replace them. It is infinitely preferable to try and pull them off as an inspection than to discover they are rotten when you grab one to stop yourself falling in the river. Pulpit and pushpit rails need to be examined for strength in the same way. Don't be afraid to give them as hard a tug as you can manage; if you were to grab them in an emergency that's

Rails need to be firmly fixed.

just what you would do, and it wouldn't be the time to worry about whether they were strong enough.

Ventilators

These deck fittings are much more important than most people believe because good ventilation is essential for a boat. It is vital to let the warm, moisture-laden air out and to allow cool dry air in, since the effect of poor ventilation is to encourage moulds and wood rots inside the cabin. Ventilators need to be cleaned at least once a year to remove the cobwebs and dust, and to ensure an uninterrupted flow of air.

Weatherproofing Cruiser Fittings

Weatherproofing small fittings such as ventilators and cleats is usually simply a matter of unscrewing the fitting, placing a bead of silicon sealant underneath it and tightening it up again. Larger fittings such as windows are a bit more trouble, and more prone to leakage.

Silicon Sealant

Modern silicon sealant is an extremely useful item on a boat because it bonds well to metal, fibreglass, wood and paint, forming a tough, flexible, waterproof seal. However, it can be awful stuff to work with if you are not familiar with its properties. It is exceptionally sticky and will get on your fingers, and then onto everything within arm's reach — and it doesn't wash off! Nevertheless, it has one property which helps: it does not stick to a wet surface.

To replace a window, proceed as follows: first, get the frame in situ, with all the screws or bolts just started, and then inject a bead of sealant into the gap between frame and boat;

next, tighten up the screws until the sealant is just beginning to be pressed out of the closing gap, and has formed a seal all the way around. At this point take a mist sprayer and lightly spray the area with water, enough to wet all the surfaces but not to cause a run-off; then when the screws are tightened up completely, the excess sealant cannot bond to the frame or the boat. Once the frame is fully tightened, leave the sealant to 'cure' for a day; then trim off any excess with a razor blade. A word of caution: silicon sealant releases acetic acid vapour as it cures; this can lightly corrode aluminium, and it certainly makes the eyes water if at all concentrated. It does therefore need to be used in a well ventilated space, although this is not usually a problem on the river.

Masts and Aerials

The nature of inland cruising tends to ensure that tall masts get shortened, sometimes the hard way. It is important that radio masts and others can be stepped down, or a low bridge will do it for you. The base-plate of a mast has to support it against surprisingly high wind forces, and in due course this can become loose. A large base-plate is essential to spread the load evenly; if the mast works loose, check that this plate is big enough, and if necessary enlarge it.

Rubbing Strakes

Inland boats spend a lot more time in intimate contact with locks, bridges, pontoons and floating fork-lift truck pallets than their sea-going counterparts, so probably it comes as no surprise that they have plenty of rubbing strakes bolted and glued onto them for extra protection. The main rubbing strip is along the edge of the gunwales, this being the widest part of the boat, and there are secondary strips around the bows and stern. The rubbing strip round the gunwales has to take a tremendous battering over the years, and often needs replacement; there are companies which specialize in making rubber and plastic strips. The rubber strips are designed to be screwed directly onto the hull, the screw heads being indented into the strip and protected by an inset strip. Hard plastic strips are screwed on in much the same way, but need to be heated in a bucket of hot water so as to make them sufficiently flexible to bend around the boat. Wooden strakes are not robust enough for use on the gunwales, not even when reinforced with aluminium.

Wooden strakes can, however, be used to protect the corners of the stern and the chines about the bows; they are frequently screwed into place from the inside, and not infrequently are ripped off by a bump. This can result in a line of small holes left beneath the waterline, and in comes the river. Where the strakes are fastened in this manner beneath the waterline around the bows, check regularly that the screws are still watertight; when they need replacing, bed the new strake on a wide band of silicon and always use stainless steel screws. It is a good idea to use hardwood for these replacements.

Canopies

One of the most expensive items on a cruiser, apart from the motor, is the cockpit canopy. These are normally made from PVC-coated canvas with clear plastic windows sewn in, supported on an aluminium or steel folding framework. We all know just how cussed they can be after a few years.

Their first weak point is the zips. These are usually hefty industrial things more suited to doing up the sides of lorries than a boat; they get stiff, the cloth backing ribbon breaks, and dirt clogs their teeth. Newer canopies tend to have Velcro fastenings which are much easier. The zips need to be kept clean and rubbed with candle wax at least once a year to keep them lubricated.

Elastic canopy ties.

The plastic windows dislike being rolled up in cold weather and promptly crack, and even if they survive this treatment for a couple of years then they go misty, and will still need replacing. Both zips and the clear plastic can be obtained from tent or caravan shops and sewn by hand into the existing place. The average sewing machine isn't nearly strong enough to cope with the thickness of the PVC: it is a matter of settling down for a long and tedious session with a leather needle and strong thimble.

The little button fasteners that are used to secure the canopy to the roof are more difficult to replace, and once they start to go the whole thing is probably on its way out. They can initially be replaced by circular grommets holding elastic stays; these then hook onto hooks screwed to the hull. These are more versatile about their placing. Besides, a

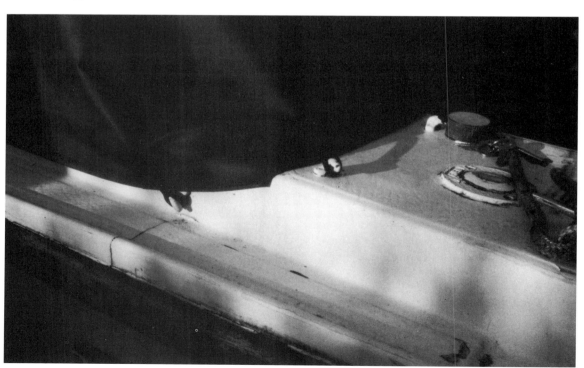

Rubber canopy ties.

canopy has quite a high degree of thermal expansion and so it cannot be rigidly fastened on all sides; some allowance has to be made for the change in dimensions with temperature. A good mixture to use would be rigid button fasteners along the top edge, and elastic rubber stays at the bottom.

The PVC material is good for a surprisingly long time. The problem is that after a few years the colour fades and it starts to look a lot worse than it really is. Since the things cost nearly five hundred pounds to replace, it isn't surprising that a company has produced a product to renew the faded surface. This is like a spray paint, but capable of bonding to the plastic surface, and is straightforward to use; as when painting, the surface needs to be thoroughly cleaned, and when completely dry, sprayed in much the same way as would a car. The spray is very powerful, to enable it to bond to the PVC; thus it will also stick very effectively and permanently to anything else you happen to spray. So if you accidentally spray someone else's canopy because of a gust of wind, be prepared for a big bill!

Hull Care Summary

The entire structure of the boat needs to be examined in detail at least once a year; this should prevent any small problem or fault reaching a stage where it could endanger the boat or the crew. Scratches and bumps resulting from the rough and tumble of inland cruising rarely result in lasting damage to a boat, and boats can almost always be repaired. Cleaning the boat regularly is one of the very best ways to keep a close watch on the structure and to notice problems arising. It is also the only way to keep the boat looking at its best, and maintaining its value as an investment.

Hull and Superstructure check-list

Monthly checks
Deck fittings, for loosening of mounting screws
Window seals (wait for a rainy day!)
Rubbing strakes, for damage
Transom brackets, for cracks and weakening
Hull, for collision damage

Monthly tasks
A good wash to remove abrasive grime
Wax polish of fibreglass
Metal polish of fittings

Annual checks
Complete detailed inspection of the entire boat for cracks and osmosis
Inspection of all deck fittings and windows for strength and weather tightness

Annual tasks
Repairs to any cracks that have occurred from collisions
Cleaning out fixed ventilators, including gas and petrol locker drain vents
Renew anti-fouling paint

— 2 —

Engines

Common Elements of Propulsion Systems

A cruiser has to have an engine of some description to be able to navigate. This is almost invariably an internal combustion engine driving a propeller through a gearbox: it can be an outboard or an inboard engine, or a combination of the two. Each design has its own special benefits and drawbacks, but they all rely on the turning propeller to thrust water away from the boat, and thus thrust the boat forwards; Newton's Law of action and reaction being equal and opposite. A further example of Newton's Law is clearly demonstrated when an outboard is used to turn a boat, where the thrust pushes the water to one side and the boat turns to the other; like Archimedes' discovery of displacement (the physicist in his bath), the physics of boats is simple enough.

The propeller will always need to transmit

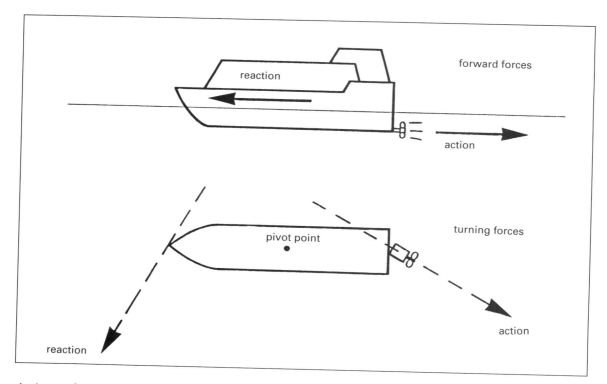

Action and reaction.

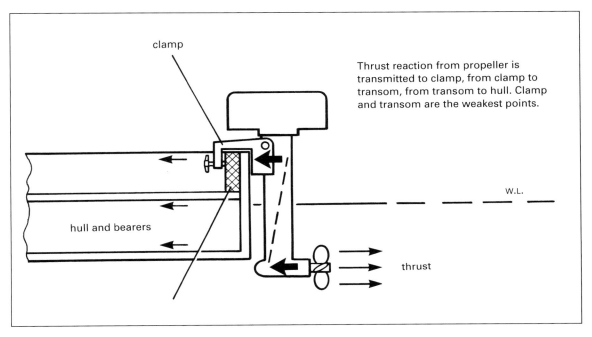

clamp

Thrust reaction from propeller is transmitted to clamp, from clamp to transom, from transom to hull. Clamp and transom are the weakest points.

W.L.

hull and bearers

thrust

Thrust diagram for an outboard motor.

Outboard motor on test.

the thrust it develops to the hull of the boat. This thrust can be quite a hefty force, particularly if the person driving has to change suddenly from full ahead to full astern. Assuming you don't want to see the engine taking off down the river on its own, it is vital to ensure this linkage is strong enough. On an outboard the thrust is initially transmitted up the outboard motor leg and is transferred to the boat through the clamp holding the motor to the transom. The transom then spreads the force to the bottom and sides of the hull.

An inboard engine with a fixed propeller transmits the force in a slightly different way: the thrust of the prop comes up the prop-shaft and into a thrust-absorbing bearing which transfers the force to large structural bearers bonded to the hull. Some inboard engines rely on the thrust from the prop-shaft being transmitted direct to the engine block, and then through the engine's feet to the hull; however, this is not a perfect solution since

'Z' drive.

it places undue strain on the engine mountings and can lead to serious vibration and premature failure of the engine mounts. Outdrives, the combination of the two, take the thrust up the outdrive leg and into the transom through the large mounting bracket.

It is worth examining all areas of the boat which are exposed to the thrust of the propeller once a year to ensure that nothing is deteriorating under the stress. Wooden transoms, either on wooden boats, or part of a GRP cruiser, can become rotten and lose their strength. If a transom fails it can be very serious, as in ripping off the back of the boat!

Control Cables

All engines have to be controlled by a mechanical linkage to the gearbox and throttle. This is normally a twin- or single-lever control at the helm, connected to the throttle and gear change on the engine block by flexible cables.

Maintenance is mostly a matter of ensuring that the cables remain adequately greased. Once a year the upper ends of the cables should be disconnected and some light oil dribbled into each one; to do this, form a cup with adhesive tape or modelling clay around the end of the outer sleeve and pour a little oil into it, as into a little reservoir, from where it can then seep down into the cable. Working the cable about will help the oil to penetrate thoroughly. It is essential that the cables are well lubricated; they will become stiff to operate and eventually break if they dry out. The ends of the cables, particularly at the motor end, are likely to attract grit and rust; this will reduce the life of a cable, so it is a good idea to wipe them all clean once a month. If the braided metal of the cable becomes frayed it is time to replace it. Outboard motor cables tend to require more attention and last less time because of the additional bending they have to do whilst steering the boat. These cables are relatively expensive, so the extra care is well worth the effort.

Outboard motor cables have quick-release clips which are often made of plastic. These will need close inspection to check that the plastic is not becoming brittle from exposure to sunlight. It is worth smearing them with a grease to keep the quick-release catch easy to work.

Steering Cables

There are several types of steering gear. Outboard motors and outdrives swivel on their own, pointing the thrust from the prop to the appropriate side; this is a very effective steering method since it only takes a small amount of lateral thrust to alter direction. Its drawback, however, is that when the power is off, the boat has little or no steering, and this is a real disadvantage when manoeuvering into a tight space. Outboards can be turned with a cable-and-pulley system, or

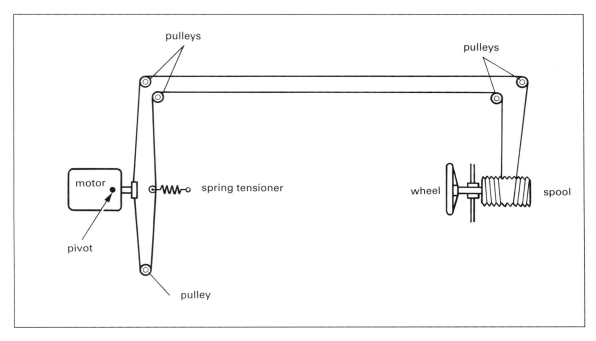

pulleys

pulleys

pulleys

motor

spring tensioner

wheel

spool

pivot

pulley

Outboard cable steering system.

Pulley and cable steering wheel.

with a much heavier duty version of the control cable. The cable-and-pulley system can be most frustrating if it goes wrong! The cables need to be examined regularly for fraying and other damage, and it is also worth checking that they are up to the job; for example, plastic-coated steel cable is the best sort of cable to use, whereas old washing lines are no good at all. Each year the pulleys need to be greased, and the springs holding the system in tension will also benefit from a coat of oil. The centre boss of the steering wheel needs lubrication, too.

Replacing a cable-and-pulley steering linkage can be a thoroughly frustrating job! Always examine, and note down, the exact location and direction of the cables before you dismantle them; replacing them should be a simple business, as long as you know where they have got to go! New cable will have a degree of play in it, so check the tension after a week of use. Due to the gearing provided by

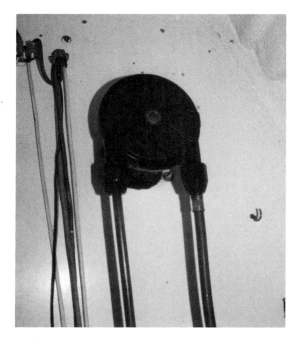

Rod-type steering gear.

the steering wheel, some quite large forces can be applied to these cables, so it is important to do up all the brackets and stays firmly.

The flexible rod-type of steering linkage is a far more satisfactory way of controlling the outboard. Most of the moving parts are enclosed in a sleeve, and the only areas that are prone to damage are the ends. A wipe over with an oily rag every month will keep the outboard end clean, and the steering wheel end will need a grease once a year. It is important to ensure that the plastic-coated sleeve is not exposed to any rough corners, as these will wear through the plastic and then water and dirt can enter the core. These units are usually used for outdrives.

Rudders

Boats with fixed propellers must have a rudder to steer. Although they are slightly less manoeuvrable than an outboard or outdrive, a rudder provides good steering when

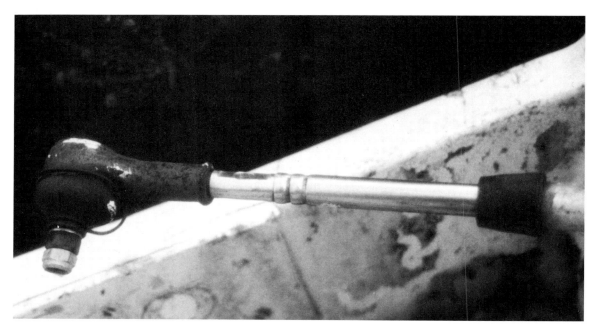

Rod-type steering gear must be kept clean (never mind the boat!).

Extension rudder for an outboard.

the motor is not supplying drive thrust. There is an assortment of bearings with which to mount the rudder on the boat, ranging from a couple of hooks screwed to the transom with a tangle of lines and pulleys, to the much more sophisticated, hydraulically operated, twin-position power-driven rudder. Mostly there is a waterproof gland bearing in the hull with a quadrant above it connected to cables, chains or flexible wire up to the helm. Whatever variety is fitted, it is most important to examine the linkages in detail at least once a year to check that everything is moving smoothly. If there is a gland through the hull below the waterline it will probably need to be greased regularly. If the boat runs aground, or suffers some other trauma to the rudder, it is crucial to examine all the rudder

linkage to check that nothing has been damaged. If the rudder linkage fails it can be very embarrassing, and you will probably end up spinning around like a drunk duck in the middle of the river. Still, that's better than walloping into someone else's boat.

Anodes

Outboard motors and the exposed metalwork of inboards and outdrives suffer from electrolytic corrosion when they are immersed in water. Basically, this is a tiny electric current generated between two dissimilar metals and the water; the metal with the highest electrochemical value tries to transfer itself to the lower electrochemical point, in a process similar to electroplating. This results in the

Even outboards need anodes.

rapid corrosion of the metal. To reduce the damage this does, most manufacturers fit sacrificial anodes to the outboard motor, to the outdrive and sometimes even to the prop-shaft brackets. These anodes are made of metal of an even higher electrochemical value, and will therefore be the first to corrode. Depending on the size of an anode and its composition, it should last between one and four years. Once half of its mass has been corroded away, it is time for replacement, and the replacement needs to be made of relatively 'correct' metal to work properly; thus anodes for one make of motor may not be the right stuff for a different make.

Trim Tabs

These are little flaps that affect the trim of a boat. Normally they are not fitted to inland cruisers because they are designed to keep a boat well trimmed when it is travelling at speed. For those who do have them fitted, it is as well to keep them in good condition as per the manufacturers' instructions.

Electrical Connections

Most cruiser engines also support an electrical system, however rudimentary. The inboard type will be based on an automotive-type alternator, and outboards will have a charging coil. The various electrical systems will be covered in a chapter on their own, but

Trim tabs are more at home at sea.

some parts of the system need to be considered in conjunction with the engine.

The electric start facility on inboard and outboard engines demands a very high current to turn the motor over, and this means that to work properly the connections between the battery and the engine block must be very clean and have minimal resistance. Even a light speckling of corrosion over the contact surfaces is enough to prevent the starter motor working. Once a year the battery terminals must be undone and cleaned thoroughly, and a smear of vaseline over the outer faces of the connector will slow down any corrosion.

All the wires from the motor to the fuseboard or dashboard will need to be checked for vibration damage at the same time. This is best done at the beginning of the season, and

if the boat is in regular use, then at least once more in the summer. Engines shake about, and the vibration weakens the copper and loosens terminals; it is certainly a tedious business checking each terminal and connector to see that it is tight and clean, but the process will ensure that the whole system is more reliable.

Petrol engines need a high voltage for the spark, and this high voltage can leak away through dirt and moisture on and around the high tension cables. These wires therefore need to be kept clean. The distributor cap on inboard engines also needs to be checked over, as it is particularly prone to condensation inside. Moisture affects the high tension side of a petrol engine very adversely: once it has created a route for the high voltage to leak to the engine block, a process

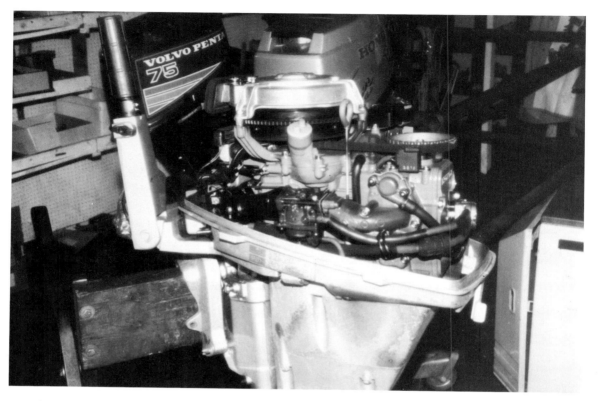

Petrol engines need to be kept clean and dry inside.

called 'tracking' starts, where the combination of the moisture and dirt along the route is turned to carbon deposits. These have a low electrical resistance, and in turn create a permanent short-circuit; the result is a motor that is unreliable.

There are water-displacing sprays available to drive excess moisture off the high tension wires; however, these are no substitute for a set of really clean and dry leads, and should only be considered as a last resort.

Diesel engines do not use electricity to fire the fuel, so they don't suffer from the same problems. However, the starter motor currents are much higher, so extra attention must be given to the condition of the wires and battery connections.

There are plenty of older cruisers around with inboard petrol engines, and many are fitted with dynamos rather than alternators: these dynamos have a fairly limited output, and the temptation to swap them for an automotive alternator is high. However, this needs to be thought through carefully. Dynamos for marine use are shrouded so that sparks generated by the brushes cannot ignite petrol vapour leaking from the carburettor. Automotive alternators are not shrouded, and so can blow the boat up! Note, too, that if the dynamo has to be replaced, the new alternator needs to be an 'ignition protected' type, as everything else in the engine compartment. All in all, inboard petrol engines have a great many ways of blowing up, and so it is vital always to ensure that the engine remains true to its original specification.

Keep fuel systems to their original specifications.

Fuel Pipe Connections

The pipework from the fuel tank to the engine needs an inspection at the very least once a year. Everything on a boat is subject to a degree of vibration and in time can be shaken to bits, and fuel pipes are equally vulnerable if not adequately secured. Since most cruisers use petrol, the consequences of a failure have the potential to be explosive. Every inch of pipework must therefore be checked visually for chafing and deterioration, and all the connectors to be sure they are not weeping even small amounts of fuel.

The flexible pipe from an outboard motor's fuel tank to the motor is particularly vulnerable to chafing against the hull. The priming bulb half-way along the pipe can also become brittle with time, and crack. Bits of dirt and rust can become trapped in the clip-on connectors, causing a fuel leak. Unlike diesel

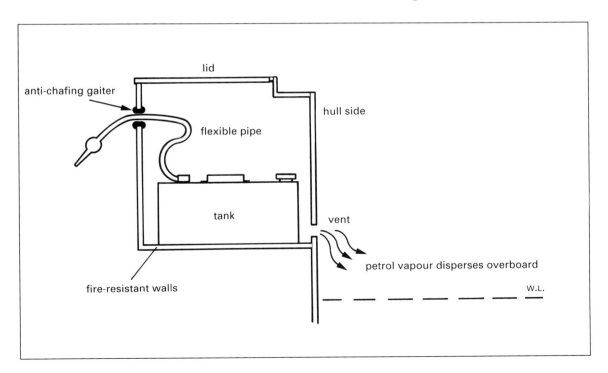

Fuel tank locker.

Petrol and gas lockers.

engines which just give up if there is the faintest trace of air entering the fuel line, a petrol engine will potter along fairly well, even though some of the fuel is in the bilges. The fuel pipes look easy enough to repair if there is a crack or a chafe mark, but remember that unless modifications to pipes are made by a qualified boat fitter, the manufacturers will deny any responsibility for subsequent problems.

Petrol is a hazardous fuel because it is so volatile; also the vapour is heavier than air and so will sink to the lowest part of the boat, the bilges, where it is difficult to disperse. It only takes a tiny spark to ignite it, and if that happens you will be looking at a hefty repair bill, and possibly a long stay in hospital. Always treat petrol with care. For example, it is important only to use petrol pipes that have been recommended by the engine manufacturer; some cheap pipes tend to go brittle

after prolonged exposure to the elements, and some connectors are not that good.

Safety First

Petrol explosions are not the only way that your engine might land you in a hospital bed. Outboard engines do not have too many exposed moving parts, but inboards do, and if your hand is trapped in the flywheel or any other moving part you will regret it. Whenever you intend to work on a motor, it is very important to ensure that it cannot start up at the wrong moment. Turn off the main battery switch so that the starter motor can't turn the engine over if someone accidentally touches the switch, and remove the spark-plug leads so there is no possibility of stray compression firing one of the cylinders. It might seem impossible to 'bump start' an engine just by turning the flywheel a little, but it has been known to happen, and this is a good way to shorten your fingers by a knuckle or two. The fuel supply should be turned off, too.

Turning off and isolating the motor may seem an unnecessary bother, especially when you are only testing it, fiddling with it a bit more, testing it again; but since the results of an accident are often permanent it surely makes sense to spend a little extra time on safety measures.

Filling the tank with petrol might not seem a dangerous thing to do, but it is one of the most frequent occasions that a boat catches fire. The main risk is when a large tank in the boat is filled from smaller cans: as the fuel is poured into the tank it displaces an equal volume of vapour out of the tank, and a bit more from evaporation, too; this vapour then sinks down to the bilges and spreads right along the bottom of the boat, and if it then happens to meet the pilot light of an appliance, or the gas flame heating up your tea . . . *Boom!* The best policy is to take the tank out of the boat to the garage and fill it there. If the tank has to be filled in the boat, double check that there are no sources of ignition available to the vapour, and thoroughly ventilate the whole boat after all the tank filler caps have been replaced, and before you even think of operating an electrical switch or lighting a cigarette.

Outboard Engines

The Two-Stroke Engine

The two-stroke engine was the obvious choice for an outboard when these were first being designed. An outboard needs to develop its power whilst weighing as little as possible, and the two-stroke cycle, which fires at every compression stroke, offered the maximum power-to-weight ratio. However, as any owner of an ageing two-stroke knows,

Two-strokes coke up plugs.

they use a lot of fuel and can be hopelessly neurotic about starting in cold weather. Modern two-strokes aren't as fussy about running, but they still use plenty of fuel. Two-strokes prefer to be run at 80 per cent of their maximum power output, and this means that they hate ticking over for hours on end. However, a high proportion of canal cruising involves just this, and so they will coke up spark plugs incessantly if not perfectly tuned.

The Four-Stroke Engine

In the last decade, four-stroke engines have been adapted very successfully for the inland waterways scene. So far they seem to have behaved impeccably, particularly as modern engines have electronic ignition and so are less prone to moisture-related problems. Four-stroke engines are much more fuel-efficient, and seem to be able to cope with prolonged running at low revs.

Four-stroke outboard motor.

The Diesel Engine

Diesel engines are not the instinctive choice for a lightweight, portable power plant. A diesel engine has to have a massive compression ratio to fire the injected fuel, and so the cylinder has to be a relatively chunky piece of engineering. Despite this limitation there are a couple of makes of diesel outboard that have provided years of reliable and economical service. It has to be said that they are slightly noisier than their petrol counterparts, but not excessively so, and they enjoy the massive advantage of being rugged and very reliable. Since a diesel engine fires on compression rather than a spark ignition, the single biggest cause of engine failure is simply not there. Moreover diesel is a much

safer fuel than petrol because it does not release an explosive vapour. One particular make of diesel outboard can also be fitted with a small hydraulic pump capable of powering other equipment such as a bow thruster or a generator, in fact almost anything you desire; I even watched one powering a heavy-duty grass cutter to clear a weed-infested canal . . . until it hit a shopping trolley.

Power Requirements

It is important to use the correct size of motor for the individual boat, and there are several factors which determine what this should be. The boat itself will need to be one factor, and a good rule of thumb is half a horsepower per foot for narrow-beam cruisers, and double

Diesel outboard powering a work-boat.

that for wide-beam; this figure will provide adequate power for most rivers and canals. The final top speed of this equation will vary according to the efficiency of the hull, but since most boats *are* reasonably efficient – unless it looks like a floating breeze block – the figure will do. However, if you intend to cruise a large river on a regular basis, and thus will need to get upstream despite the fact that it's been raining for a week and the ducks are doing 40mph downstream, choose double the size engine. It is worth seeking professional advice on this however, as you may exceed the strength of the transom; outboard motor sales staff will be able to provide specific advice.

Another factor which contributes to the power available from an outboard, and a much overlooked one, is the propeller. All major manufacturers can provide a choice of propeller, and in some cases the propellers of

one make are interchangeable with another. The motor may be running perfectly, but if it is fitted with a propeller of the wrong pitch, all the power is wasted and the fuel economy suffers badly. Propeller choice is something of a black art, the governing factors being principally the normal speed of the boat, the weight of the boat and the hull type. An authorized agent will be able to phone his head office and ask them to run a computer program to choose the optimum prop – yes, it really *is* that complicated!

Mounting Requirements

Outboards seem simple enough to mount, just screw them onto the transom and off you go . . . many would say there is a little more to it than that! Nevertheless, one of the chief causes of difficult starting is that the depth of water over the prop is too great; this then

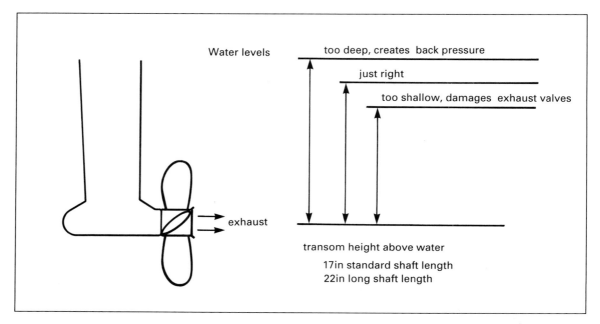

Exhaust port depth.

creates a back pressure on the exhaust port, effectively choking the engine. Outboard motors are built with different lengths of leg: thus short shaft motors are normally used on small boats like dinghies, long shaft are more usual for cruisers, and extra long for yachts. If an extra long shaft motor is put on a dinghy, the exhaust port will be 8in (20cm) further under the water than it was designed to be, and the resulting water pressure will upset the motor considerably.

The leg of the motor needs to be vertical whilst the boat is under way, and there is an adjustment on the mounting bracket to set this. Note that vertical when under way is not always the same as vertical when stationary: quite a few boats are shaped so that the bow rises up with increasing speed, and this alteration in angle will affect the outboard. In normal cruising the difference in angle is small, but if you are trying to make headway against a fast current the engine will be working flat out and the water speed may be

enough to tilt the boat quite markedly away from its normal trim. And the further away from vertical the propeller moves, the less efficient the drive will be.

Outboards are easy to mount and dismount, and this makes them very vulnerable to theft: all insurance companies therefore insist that some form of anti-theft device is fitted to the mounting bracket to foil thieves. This is normally some form of cover across the mounting screws which prevents them being undone. A padlock across the two isn't good enough, since a thief will simply knock out the retaining pins.

Fuel Tanks

The fuel tank for an outboard engine normally holds five or ten gallons (23 or 45 litres), at least enough for a couple of days' cruising. Recently the Boat Safety Scheme has introduced a number of standards to which the tank must adhere, the problem

Outboards need good ventilation.

being that any fault with the fuel storage system is likely to lead to a life-threatening situation. Basically any fuel tank must comply with the manufacturers' specification: if it does this, it will meet the Boat Safety Scheme's requirements, too.

Service Guides

On the whole, modern outboards are extremely reliable and economical engines, providing years of service; they are a far cry from those heady days of lawn-mower engines stuck onto a bit of scaffold tube. Yet there has been a price to pay for this modern reliability: nowadays an outboard engine is completely out of bounds as regards amateur repairs – if anything more serious than a fouled spark plug occurs then it must be sent to an authorized dealer and a professional must do the work on it. There are special tools

needed for most jobs nowadays, and a pair of mole-grips just won't do.

Hopefully, most engines will not need any work done on them for years, as long as they are treated correctly. The single most important task which can be done to keep a motor happy is to use it regularly. Motors are built to run, not to rust away on the back of the boat. If you can't use the motor for a couple of months, especially over the winter, then it is a very good idea to dismount it from the boat and store it upright in a dry shed or garage. This will prevent the water corroding it, and keep it safe from theft. The engine's manual will have a list of the servicing tasks you can carry out yourself, and these should be carried out scrupulously to maintain the engine at peak performance.

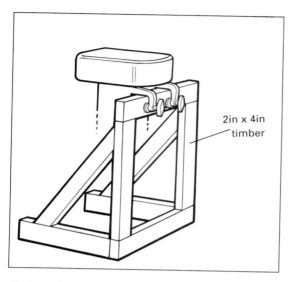

2in x 4in
timber

Outboard motor storage stand.

Common Problems

The most frequent reason for an outboard motor to break down is that the spark plugs have sooted up. This is closely followed by over-heating caused by blocked water inlets. Two-strokes are prone to the former, and any engine can suffer from the latter, though more recently some manufacturers of plugs have introduced new types which seem to coke up more slowly than the older varieties. They cost more, of course, but because they have a smaller electrode they stay so hot that the carbon doesn't form on it so readily.

There are small spark-plug cleaners available from auto-accessory shops; this is like a miniature sand-blaster, with a 12-volt motor. The sand has to be kept very dry for it to flow freely through the little blast pump. For those who have an old two-stroke that simply plasters the plugs with soot, this is an invaluable little tool. It does extend the life of a plug quite markedly, but it is important to ensure that the plug is completely free of the sand before putting it back in the engine. Modern two-strokes, with their sophisticated oil injection systems, should not foul up the plugs, and they will need professional attention if this does start to happen. Four-strokes should also keep their plugs clean, and if sooting becomes a problem, they will need to be checked by a dealer too.

Sometimes sooting of the plugs can arise because the engine is not working at its optimum revs, and this is frequently because the propeller pitch is incorrect or the motor is too big for the boat. A high fuel consumption or sluggish response are both indications that this may be the case. If you suspect the problem might be caused by propeller pitch, then it will be worth seeing a dealer and asking his advice. Propellers are expensive items, so if the dealer can be persuaded to let you try out a prospective propeller first, so much the better. As I mentioned before, propeller choice is a black art, and experimenting with different size pitches can often be more successful than relying on the computer.

Outboard motors are cooled by sucking in the river water, passing it through the engine block, and then mixing it with the exhaust gases as they are expelled. This makes for a quiet-running engine, but one that is prone to blockage. Almost all outboards are fitted with a 'Tell-Tale', a little jet of water which emerges from the casing where it is easily visible; if the water stops coming out, then you know there is a blockage and can stop the motor to remove the obstruction. This system is completely useless, however, if your motor is mounted on the back of a cruiser where you can't see it, in which case a second method of alarm is needed. A few new motors are fitted with an audible buzzer to indicate overheating, and if they are not, it is possible to buy an electronic alarm that will react in the same way. They are not expensive and since they may save you the cost of a new motor, they must be considered a wise investment.

Water in the fuel can sometimes become something of a problem. It is easy enough to clean a portable tank, and well worth using a

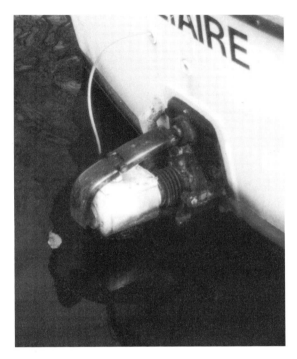

Inboard/outboard motor.

funnel with a fine water-trapping filter when filling the tank.

The worst problem an outboard motor can face is being owned by someone who fails to have it properly serviced once a year.

Inboard Engines

Inboard engines tend to be used on larger cruisers. Most of them are marine versions of automotive engines made by companies such as Ford or Peugeot. The engine block is more or less the same as that found in a car, but with a different gearbox, exhaust, cooling and electrical systems. Ideally the engine block will simply have to generate the power, and not have to absorb the thrust from the prop, but in many cases it has to do both. Inboard engines are normally much easier to work on and to service because they are not built to a

weight limit, so everything can be laid out on a larger scale. One of their drawbacks, however, is that the engineer has to come to the motor, rather than vice versa, which invariably means a larger bill.

Inboards are usually a lot more powerful than outboards, and so can provide many more extras; their electrical output is considerably larger, which allows far more equipment to be run. The cooling system can provide central heating and hot water, too. The nature of the built-in fuel tank means that they can carry more fuel, and thus have a larger range.

The Petrol Inboard Engine

Petrol inboards are gradually being replaced by diesel units. This is because the explosive nature of petrol has engendered a whole host of rules and regulations designed to reduce the risk of fires. Complying with these new rules has meant major and expensive alterations to some boats, so for those whose petrol inboard is approaching the geriatric, it would be wise to consider replacing it with a diesel engine. Petrol engines and moisture are a bad mix; condensation on the high tension leads and system can develop into starting problems, these problems can then lead to petrol vapour wafting around the engine compartment, and then it only takes a spark to really spoil your insurance company's day. Insurance companies will not view a claim for damage very favourably if the motor hasn't been looked after correctly, and unless all work carried out on it has been done in accordance with the original specification and by qualified personnel.

The Diesel Engine

Diesel engines may be heavier, noisier and much more fussy about fuel cleanliness, but at least they don't blow you into the middle of next week by accident. In fact modern diesels are much quieter than their predecessors and, to be honest, are more or less directly comparable with petrol engines. Since the compression ignition system needs no electricity they tend to be far more reliable in boats than petrol engines, and they are much more fuel-efficient. They don't really like starting in very low temperatures, but then it is unlikely that anyone will be wanting a cruise if the river is three feet of solid ice.

Diesel engines are extremely fussy about their fuel. Diesel itself is a much more viscous fluid than petrol, but it has to be injected into the cylinder as a fine mist; the slightest contamination will clog up these injectors and thus stop the engine. The compression of a diesel engine is several times greater than a petrol engine, which means that the cylinder barrels are made of stronger stuff, the injector pipes have to cope with fuel at immensely high pressure, and the injector pumps, piston rings and so on need to be machined to very fine tolerances. On the whole it is a miracle they work; but work they do, and very well.

Power Requirements

Inboard engines are most often used in wide-beam cruisers since there is more room to fit them; it can be something of a squeeze fitting an inboard into a narrow-beam cruiser. The overall weight and required speed obviously decide the exact choice, but one or two horsepower per foot length should be more than adequate for most river and canal use. Installing too large an engine is a waste of money and fuel.

Service Guides

Every engine has its own individual service

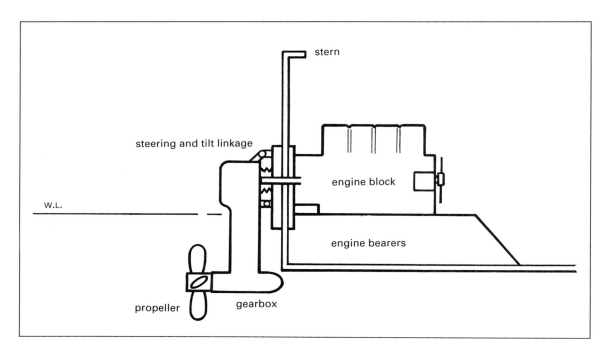

Stern drive.

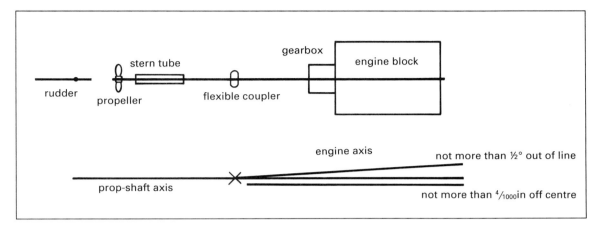

Fixed propeller engine alignment.

requirements, and these will be found in the engine's handbook. It is worth remembering that if an engine has stood idle for a year after it was serviced, it will need another service. Time passed as well as hours run affect the need for oil changes and filter changes, and every engine will need a full service at least once a year regardless of the hours clocked up running. To get the best from the engine it is worth doing the major service just before the main cruising season starts, in March, say, and a second smaller service and check-over in late autumn before the winter. This latter check-up is particularly important for boats with a raw water cooling system.

Engine Alignment

Inboard engines shake their engine mounts about enough for them occasionally to come loose. Inboards powering outdrives are normally fixed in relation to the outdrive leg, and should not get out of alignment, but engines driving a fixed propeller will need to be aligned exactly to the prop-shaft.

This alignment will need to be within half a degree along the length, and within $^4/_{1000}$ in from centre: if the engine moves more than

this much away from its correct position it will create stress and wear on the stern tube and engine mounts, leading to premature failure. A simple way to check this is to see how freely the propeller turns. If the engine is out of line it will force the prop-shaft against the side of the stern tube, creating friction. Turn off and isolate the engine so that it cannot be started, and place it in neutral. Now try to turn the propeller by hand: it should turn reasonably easily if everything is well lined up. If there are any stiff points in the circle then this probably means there is a small bend in the shaft; and if the whole thing is really hard to move then the engine is almost certainly out of line. Re-establishing the correct alignment is a tedious business: it involves either slackening off all the mounts and using a feeler gauge around the edge of the coupler; or an alternative method is to suspend the motor from an engine hoist so that it is held in position by the prop-shaft and coupler, with the hoist taking all the weight. The mounts can then be done up carefully so that the weight is taken off the hoist evenly. It is very fiddly, and great care must be taken to ensure the engine doesn't move, or even drop off, during the process; a couple of hundredweight of engine on your foot is no joke.

Gearboxes

Marine gearboxes for modern engines require little maintenance, just an oil change every now and then, depending on how much the boat is used. They are the first thing to suffer from a mis-alignment of the engine, however, and the lateral forces imposed on them by poor alignment will tear their bearings apart. They are not cheap, so it is worth checking the alignment is right at least once a year. If the propeller has taken a knock, or tried eating the stern rope, it is important to check immediately that no damage has occurred to the shaft; even a slightly bent shaft will rapidly destroy the gearbox.

Older mechanical gearboxes are more robust, but they need to have their oil level checked more regularly. These mechanical gearboxes are not really suitable for cable-type control levers, as the force needed to change gear will rapidly wear out the cable.

Exhaust Systems

Wet Exhaust Systems

Most inboards use a wet exhaust system, where the cooling water output combines with the exhaust gases to cool and muffle the smell and noise of the exhaust. The system needs to be checked at least once a month for any deterioration of the pipes. The couplings around the junction of water and exhaust manifolds need to be watched particularly carefully, as these suffer the highest vibration.

Dry Exhaust Systems

Dry exhaust systems are simpler, although noisier, the exhaust gases simply passing from the manifold through a silencer box and out to the fresh air. The pipes will need to be insulated with a heat-resistant lagging to prevent any nasty burns should anyone happen to brush against them. The flexible sections of pipe will need to be checked every now and again to ensure that they are not rusting, or cracking up under the vibration. If the silencer box rusts through it should be easy enough to replace with a new unit from a dealer.

Cooling Systems

Raw Water Systems

This is the original cooling system for inboard engines. It involves drawing water through a sea-cock in the hull, passing it through a coarse filter, and then through the engine and out again. It is a simple system, but very prone to blockages, and it has generally been superseded by a twin system using a heat exchanger so that the fluid in the engine block is kept separate and cooled via a heat exchanger. Raw water systems were developed at sea, where the water isn't quite so full of weed and junk; on canals and rivers they are a liability, clogging up with monotonous regularity. Their other weak point is that the water in the engine block cannot be treated with antifreeze and so the engine must be scrupulously drained down before frosty weather.

Heat Exchangers

The evolution of the raw water system into the modern cooling system was rapid. The cooling fluid of the engine was pumped through a heat exchanger, and the river water passed through that in order for the surplus heat to be extracted. The heat exchanger is designed so that any surplus river water drains off freely when the engine is turned off, the bore of the pipe being large enough to allow most water-borne debris to pass straight through. Best of all, it allows the

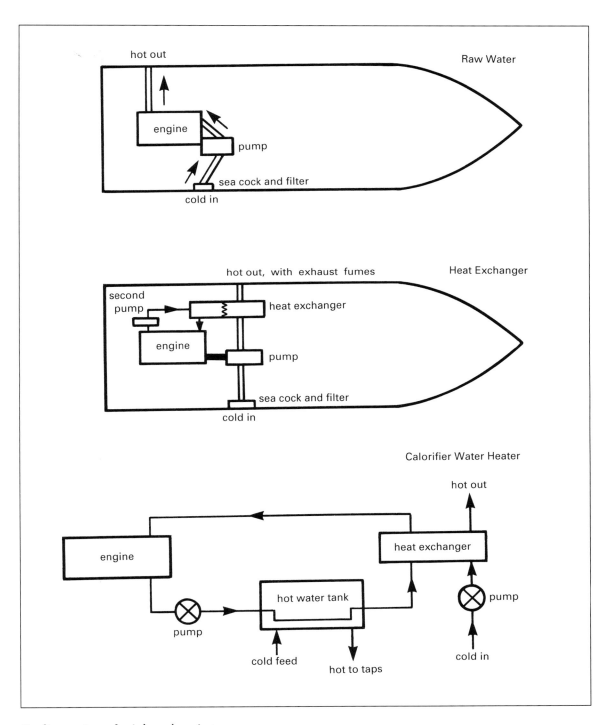

Cooling systems for inboard engines.

Raw water for cooling must be filtered.

set. It is always worth keeping a few spare lengths on board in case of an unexpected failure. Hoses are normally secured with jubilee clips; ideally these should be stainless steel ones, but they are quite likely to be of galvanized or mild steel. If this is the case, replace them with stainless steel ones as soon as possible.

Air-Intake Filters

Air filters for marine engines tend to be rather lightweight affairs, largely because there is very little dust at sea. It isn't quite the same for inland navigation, however, and a good air filter will prolong the engine's life. It is therefore important not to neglect the air filter change during an engine's service. Some engines have a dry filter, and others use a wet (oiled) filter; whichever sort it is, look after it, and it will look after the engine.

Summary

Cruisers have such a variety of different engines that it is difficult to specify a maintenance schedule that will cover every eventuality. It is therefore important for every cruiser owner to find out the manufacturer's guidelines relevant to his own engine, and to follow them specifically. An engine is the heart of the boat, providing power for travel, heating and lighting. If it is used and looked after well it should be capable of providing decades of reliable service; under-used and poorly serviced it will become nothing more than an expensive chunk of scrap-metal. An unreliable engine is a liability because it could fail at a critical moment, for example by a weir, and thus endanger the lives of everyone on board. A modern engine is a fairly complicated machine and needs to be mended and adjusted by properly qualified engineers. The days of belting it with a big hammer are long gone!

engine cooling section to contain antifreeze and corrosion inhibitors.

Both of these types of cooling rely on a water intake below the waterline of the hull, an intake which is via a well maintained sea-cock that can be closed readily in the event of a hose rupturing. This sea-cock needs to be checked and operated regularly to ensure it is always ready for use. Both systems should then be fitted with a coarse-mesh filter which will catch the worst of the debris. This filter will need to be cleaned every day that the motor is run, and sometimes even more often than that, depending on the quality of the water.

The hoses need to be checked visually at least once a week, and very thoroughly once a year. They are prone to chafing and attack by petrol and diesel, and if they fail they could sink the boat. If a hose leaves a black mark on your finger when you rub it, it is time to start thinking about getting a replacement

---

Cruising Maintenance Schedule

Daily Care (where applicable)
Check sump oil level
Check fuel level
Check two-stroke oil level
Grease stern tube
Clean water-intake filter
Check coolant level

Weekly care
All of the above, plus:
Battery electrolyte levels
Alternator drive belt tension
Gearbox oil level
Engine mountings
Control cables and steering system
Check wiring loom for visual faults
Check water hoses for leaks

Annual Care
(regardless of hours cruised in the year)
Complete service of the engine and transmission system
Change or clean all fuel and coolant filters
Detailed inspection of all electrical wires and connections
Detailed inspection of fuel tanks and pipes
Check engine alignment
Check integrity of exhaust systems
Check thrust-absorbing areas of the hull

— 3 —

Trailers

A trailer is an invaluable addition to a small cruiser's equipment. It opens up an entirely new world of exploration, enabling you to take your cruiser not only onto other waterways around Britain, but also onto the continent. A trailer also allows the boat to be stored ashore over winter, or indeed whenever it is not being used, thus saving a small fortune in mooring fees.

Trailers are rather expensive, and secondhand ones are as rare as hens' teeth, so it pays to look after them. A handful of trailer manufacturers in the UK can provide a kit of parts for home assembly, or a ready-built unit. For those contemplating buying a new one, it is worth checking that the steelwork is fully galvanized and rust-proofed, that the overrun brakes have an automatic reversing facility, and that the winch has enough strength to haul the weight of your boat up the rollers. A boat trailer needs a great many rollers to spread the weight evenly across the hull.

Home-assembly trailer kits used to be a cheap option since they allowed the builder to scrounge hubs and wheels from a scrap yard to save costs. This practice is now

Trailers provide the freedom to explore new waters.

frowned on, and a new trailer needs to be fitted with new wheels and hubs. Boat trailers are submerged into canals and rivers so often that cheap old car hubs will rust away to nothing very quickly.

Choosing a Trailer

There are a few points to consider before you contemplate investing in a trailer.

The Boat

Boats over 22ft (6.6m) long are unlikely to be suitable for much long-distance travelling, mainly because they are so heavy that a very hefty car is needed to drag them about. Boats over 8ft 6in (2.5m) wide are considered to be a 'wide load', and face special restrictions.

Weight

Cars can only tow so much weight, and normally the combined weight of the boat and trailer should not exceed 85 per cent of the kerbside weight of the car. If it does, the stability of the car/trailer rig will be adversely affected.

The Car

A car can only pull so much. Different makes of car are designed with different performance criteria: thus some cars can develop their peak power at relatively low speeds, which makes them good for towing, but not so brilliant at speed; whilst other cars are high-revving speed machines that might zip past you on the motorway, but couldn't pull the skin off a rice pudding. For those who have one of these speed machines, don't expect the poor thing to do a hill start with a cabin cruiser on the back; hill starts are rather common when pulling boats around, in fact every time you use a slipway.

The Correct Balance

Car manufacturers specify what their vehicle is capable of achieving, what it weighs and what it can tow. To achieve optimum performance when pulling a boat and trailer, the balance between towed weight and towing vehicle needs to be correct. Naturally the lighter the towed weight the easier life will be, but boats are generally fairly heavy, and pulling a cruiser will probably be taxing the car to its limits. It is important not to exceed these limits, legally as well as from a survival point of view: if the car has to pull more than its own weight the rig can become unstable. Pulling the boat up a hill is one problem, having it shove your car all the way down the other side is an altogether more serious matter.

The car has what is known as a kerbside weight: this is the weight of the car without passengers or luggage, but with a full tank of fuel. The boat and trailer together form the 'trailer weight', and if you are in any doubt about this, take the trailer to a public weighbridge and get it weighed: this is important, because the car manufacturer specifies a 'gross train weight' which is the most that the car is designed to cope with. If you add the kerbside weight and the trailer weight together, and subtract this total from the gross train weight, the figure left over is the weight of luggage and passengers you can squeeze into the car.

It is normal practice to remove as much weight from the boat as possible and to stow it in the car. Ideally the boat should weigh as little as possible for towing; only under exceptional circumstances should it weigh more than the car, and drivers need to be experienced if this is the case. A poorly balanced rig will be prone to weaving and generally misbehaving at speed.

In addition to balancing the weight between the car and trailer, it is necessary to balance the tow hitch of the trailer so that it

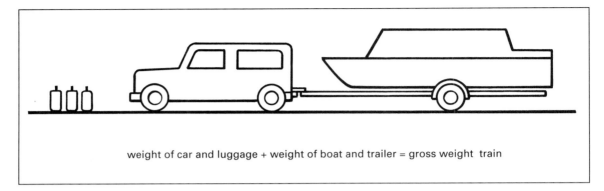

weight of car and luggage + weight of boat and trailer = gross weight train

Gross train weight.

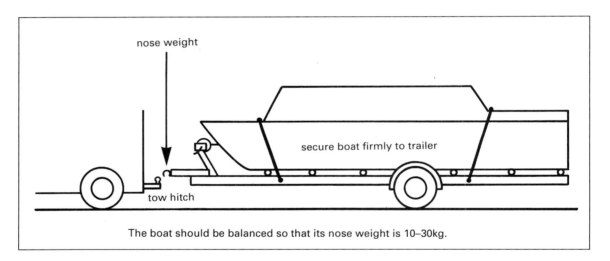

nose weight

secure boat firmly to trailer

tow hitch

The boat should be balanced so that its nose weight is 10–30kg.

Trailer balance is very important.

has a weight of about ten to thirty kilograms (22 to 66lb). This is achieved by carefully positioning the boat over the axle. This nose-weight varies from vehicle to vehicle and the preference of the driver; weight positioned higher makes for a more steady and stable ride, although the tow hitch can only take so much static load. Note that high nose-weight on the rear of the car can also push it down so much that the front comes up. The effect of this is to lose traction and steering as the front wheels are lifted from the road. The headlamp alignment is ruined, too.

Weaving

If the trailer is incorrectly balanced it is prone to weave about above a certain speed. For those new to towing, it can come as a very nasty shock to find 'the tail wagging the dog'. Poor balance and excessive speed are the causes, but what to do once it starts? *Do not* slam on the brakes! And *do not* try and out-accelerate the sway. The technique is to slacken off the power gently, allowing the car and trailer to slow down gradually on the engine overrun. Only apply the brakes, and

Some Common Boats, and their Original Weights

Under 1 ton

	kilos		kilos
Shetland 460	420	Shetland Sea Lark	250
Microplus 501	345	Microplus 561	705
Birchwood 18	703	Birchwood Continental	617
Dawncraft Dandy	499	Domino 16	267
Marina 19	609	Tri-Star	204
Europa 4	432	Landor 17	408
Fairline 20	711	Dolphin 20	864
Camargue 16	250	Capri 160	272
Yeoman 16	272	Safari 610	635
Yeoman 21	680		

1–2 tons

	kilos		kilos
Vixen Mk II	1,016	Buckingham 20	1,016
Freeman 6/10	1,425	Freeman 23	1,524
Nauticus 22	1,360	Nauticus 27	1,814
Dobson 24	1,388	Dolphin 23	1,625
Dolphin 24	1,220	Dawncraft 25	1,626
Trentcraft 25	1,650	Buckingham 25	1,524
Conway 26	1,815	Interceptor 25	1,860

Over 2 tons

	kilos		kilos
Fairline Fury	2,032	Chriscraft 25	2,324
Princess 25	2,016	Seamaster 813	2,286
Seamaster 8m	3,048	Cleopatra 850	3,175
Harrier 850	4,082	Ocean 30	6,096
Seamaster 30	4,064		

then very gently, if you are going downhill. The steering wheel will jump a bit with each sway, but don't fight it or try to over-compensate, because it will ease off as the weave settles down. Once the outfit has stopped weaving you will know what speed to avoid in future. It may be that the balance of the trailer has shifted during the journey and needs some adjustment.

Trailer Maintenance

The Chassis

The chassis of a galvanized steel trailer shouldn't require much attention. It will need a visual inspection once a year to check that there are no cracks or bends developing in the steel; these are likely to appear if the trailer is overloaded, and the most usual

Try to keep the trailer in its original condition.

spots are around the suspension unit brackets and the winch post. Ordinary steel trailers will require quite a lot more attention because of their liability to rust. Boat trailers are frequently made of box-section steel, and once these have got wet inside, they rust from the inside out. It is easy enough to paint the outside, but there is not a great deal one can do about the inside. If the rust has not progressed too far it is a good idea to use a wax-based, rust-prevention spray which can be injected all the way down the box section and should be good for about three to four years, depending on the number of immersions. An ungalvanized trailer needs a proper paint treatment to stop the rust; this is in addition to all the drips of anti-fouling that it will be plastered with sooner or later.

The Winch

A heavy duty winch on a trailer is really

essential. Most slipways are sloped so that the boat will get most of the way onto the trailer, but the winch will be needed to pull the boat up the last few feet. If this winch is

The winch.

not looked after it can be dangerous, because if the cable breaks whilst it is under load it will lash about like a snake, with vicious results. Every year the cable must be fully unwound and checked closely to see that it isn't fraying anywhere. A good wipe over and coat of oil will keep it free running and rust free. The winch gears and moving parts need to be greased, and the catches and brakes tested. All the clamps securing the cables must be inspected, too. A good winch mechanism will last a lifetime, but the cable may need replacing from time to time. If a kink or a knot appears in the wire it will weaken the cable and it should be replaced. This isn't too expensive, fortunately.

Tyres and Wheels

Trailer tyres suffer from problems that are not experienced on cars. They may not do a high mileage, but they are very prone to ageing and although the tread can appear perfect, the side walls deteriorate rapidly if not looked after well. The main cause of failure is that the tyres are left for months, sometimes even years, in one place; the permanent pressure on the tyre is thus not distributed evenly by the usual rotation, and this leads to bulges in the side walls and eventual failure. Nevertheless, there are certain precautions that will double or treble the life of tyres: the first of these is to remove the pressure from them whilst the trailer is out of use. The trailer can be jacked up so that the wheels are just off the ground, and supported on a stack of breeze blocks at each corner. Partially reducing the air pressure will also ease the process of ageing. If this isn't an option, it is a good idea to mark the tyres with a few chalk marks, and once a month move the trailer so that the load is placed on a different part of the wheel each time.

Tyres also suffer degradation from sunlight and ozone. Ozone isn't a problem inland, but near the sea it can have a marked effect on

tyres over a long period. If the tyres are wrapped up in an old sheet this will prevent the ozone getting close to the rubber. It will also prevent the sunlight hitting the tyres.

The wheels of a trailer should not suffer from damage in normal circumstances. However, it is still worth checking them once a year to make sure there are no dents or buckles that may cause them to shed the tyre.

Twin-Axle Trailers

Trailers with two axles suffer from increased wear on the tyres. The closer together the axles are, the less the wear, but either the front or the back axle will get dragged sideways when the trailer turns, and this dragging will cause uneven wear on the tyres. This uneven wear can be felt if you slide your hand across the tread: it will feel smooth one

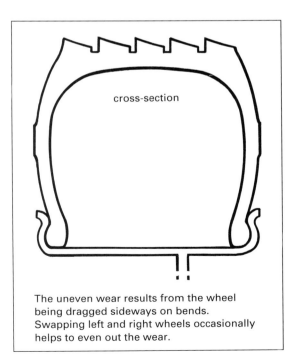

The uneven wear results from the wheel being dragged sideways on bends. Swapping left and right wheels occasionally helps to even out the wear.

Tyre wear caused by twin-axle trailer.

way and rough the other. Swapping the wheels around periodically will help to even out the wear.

Wheel Bearings

The wheel bearings of a boat trailer have to carry a lot of weight, and are regularly submersed, so they usually wear out quite quickly. It is always worth getting the best quality you can afford, and make sure that they are always packed with a high melting-point grease. If the bearing has a grease nipple, it is worth pumping a bit more in each time the trailer comes out of the water as this will displace any moisture that may have seeped into the bearing. Wheel bearings become hot if they are stressed, and it is worth checking that they are not over-heating during a journey.

Before any long journey it is worth checking that the bearings are tight. To do this, jack up the trailer and try to wobble the wheel. It should turn freely around, but have no movement in any other direction, up or down, or

side to side. Some bearings have an adjustment to take up any slack as the bearing rollers wear away, and some don't. The former are simple enough to tighten: remove the hub cover, take out the split pin securing the large castellated nut and tighten it until the wheel will not revolve, then slacken it off by two notches. The wheel should now turn freely, but with no other movement. Replace the split pin with a new one and repack the hub with grease. Don't forget to replace the cap. Non-adjustable bearings have to be replaced if they are worn.

The bearings will need a complete overhaul and inspection about every two thousand miles (3,200km). They will need to be completely taken apart, washed in solvent to remove any grit, and checked for wear. The oil seals will need to be checked, too. If they look suspect, replace them. This sort of work could have dreadful consequences if it is not done correctly, so for those who don't feel qualified to do it, take the trailer down to the local garage and arrange for them to check it over.

Brakes

Most boat trailers have overrun brakes, activated by a linkage on the hitch: if the mass of the trailer starts to push against the tow hitch, it compresses a ram which pulls the brakes on. It is an elegant and simple system which is not prone to failure if well maintained. Older systems have normal car hubs and cables to pull the brakes on; modern systems have an automatic reversing facility, and rods rather than cables.

There should be a hydraulic damper on the tow-hitch end to prevent the brakes working at the slightest bump; a handbrake; and on the old braking systems there is usually a lever of some description which will stop the brakes locking when reversing: the effect of reversing the trailer is just the same as slowing down whilst travelling, and activates the

Keep the bearings well lubricated.

brakes. There is a linkage from here to the brake drums, inside which is a pivot that expands the shoes outwards to grip the drum and thus slow the trailer.

Let us start at the drawbar of the brake activator: this should slide in and out with a degree of resistance because of the damper. Most makes require greasing, and have a nipple on the housing to inject the grease. The handbrake lever will need its hinge greasing, as will the reversing lock out-lever. The handbrake adjustment will usually indicate if the brake linings are worn: if it is nearing the limit of its adjustment, they probably are. If the trailer is fitted with cables rather than rods, it may mean that the cable has stretched. Behind this are the rods to the brake assemblies; all the connectors and hinges on these need to be greased so that everything is operating smoothly.

To check the internal workings of the brake drums, the trailer needs to be jacked up and supported on axle stands, and the wheels removed. The brake drum is then accessible. It is normally removed by undoing a retaining screw on the outside face and gently tapping it and pulling. Make sure that the brakes are not on at the time, since they will prevent it moving. Brake liners contain asbestos dust, so it is essential to wear a face mask. Inside, the dust will probably have coated everything, and this needs to be cleaned away.

The brake shoes should appear to be in good condition. However, they do tend to expand and deteriorate if they are left wet for any length of time, and this will lead to high spots and possibly even delamination, when the lining starts to flake off. High spots can be filed down, but delamination is cause for replacement. The leading edges may need to be chamfered. The shoes will need replacing if they have worn down to less than ⅛in (3mm) if it is a bonded shoe, and before it becomes flush with the rivets on a riveted shoe. Never allow a riveted shoe to wear right down to the rivets because they will score the brake drum and ruin it.

The pivots and levers will need a smear of grease on their working surfaces; the drum will need a good clean as well. When it is reassembled, the brakes should be adjusted by tightening the adjuster until they just start to bite, and then backing off one turn. When the wheels are replaced it is worth taking the trailer for a drive around the block to check all is working correctly.

Automatic reversing brakes come in a variety of types, and each has specific extra maintenance needs and methods of adjustment. Use their maintenance manual to provide the correct adjustment for them. As with bearing replacement, if you feel you are not qualified to carry out the work, take the trailer to a garage.

Tow Hitch

The tow-hitch ball and socket need to be cleaned and regreased once a year to prevent an accumulation of grit ruining the smooth surfaces of the ball and the socket. At the same time it is worth checking the attachment points on the vehicle to make sure they are not working loose. The electrical socket and trailer-board plug will need a clean, and the contacts can be brightened up with a bit of emery cloth at the same time. The trailer-board cable will need to be inspected for damage as it is prone to being trapped between the boat and trailer and thus broken.

Suspension Systems

These require very little maintenance. Most boat trailers have sealed steel in rubber torsion bar units that cannot be adjusted. Older trailers may have coil springs with hydraulic dampers, or leaf springs. The coil springs and hydraulic dampers are sealed for life, so do not need anything; leaf springs require a good clean and lubrication once a year.

Trailer Lighting Requirements

It is important that a trailer lighting board is secured to the back of the trailer or boat when travelling on the road; it must also meet current DoT regulations. Boards are available cheaply enough from most auto shops. However, they are not usually fitted with a long enough lead to reach from the car's electrical towing socket to the back of the boat, so an extension lead will need to be either bought or made to make up the distance. Testing these boards is simplicity itself: place the board on the windscreen of the car and test the indicators and lights as you sit in the driving seat; it couldn't be easier to see! If you are on a long journey and want to check that it is all working without getting out, find a big shop window and manoeuvre the rig until you can see the reflection of the trailer board, if you can do so without inconveniencing other road users.

Securing the Boat

The boat needs to be firmly secured to the trailer in transit; it will be travelling a lot faster than it does on the water! It will also be shaken fairly violently if the road is rough or bumpy. Nylon webbing cargo straps with tensioners are the best method of fixing the boat; these are incredibly strong and will not stretch and slacken half-way along a motorway. Good quality ropes are serviceable, but take a lot longer to fix. Remember that the shape of the boat can cause ties to slip forwards or backwards and lose their tension. Inside the boat things will be rattled about, and it is a good policy to stow everything movable in the towing vehicle, not simply to reduce the weight of the boat, but to prevent it all ending up in a broken pile on the floor.

Larger outboard motors cannot simply be removed and stowed in the boot, and will need to be left in situ. If this is the case the propeller has to be covered because it is classed as a sharp object; special bags can be bought to protect it.

Petrol and water tanks are best carried empty; they can always be filled up at your destination. There isn't much point in taking large boxes of groceries for the same reason. It all adds weight to the vehicle, and when towing a heavy boat, the old adage about travelling light takes on a whole new meaning.

Summary

A boat trailer provides new horizons for the owner of a small boat, but it must be maintained meticulously because if it breaks down it may cause a catastrophe. And it is all too easy to stow a trailer in a corner and then forget it until you next need it. The speeds which a vehicle towing a boat can achieve are considerable, and this places unusual and powerful strains on both trailer and towing vehicle, and to a certain extent the boat, too. Practice is the key to successful towing, along with good maintenance.

Check-list for Annual Inspection

Tow-hitch and ball: clean and re-grease
Electrical system: check and clean contacts if needed
Brake activator ram: check for proper movement; grease
Brake linkages: check for stretch; grease
Brake linings: check for wear
Handbrake: adjust for correct action
Rollers and winch: check for free play; grease
Winch cable: check for fraying
Suspension: check for proper movement
Chassis: check for rust and distortion

— 4 —

Plumbing and Gas Systems

Plumbing Systems

Plumbing systems on cruisers are usually simple affairs, the space restrictions being such that there is only room for a small water tank, a sink and a toilet. On many cruisers there is barely room for a shower, and baths are generally out of the question. Plumbing systems require very little maintenance if they have been installed correctly.

Water tanks

There are several varieties of tank suitable for cruisers, and one that is definitely not suitable. If your boat has a glass-fibre section of the hull for a water tank it must have been built in by the manufacturer, otherwise it will allow water to penetrate the laminate of the GRP and this will cause osmosis.

Water tanks need to be big enough to hold sufficient water for at least a couple of days cruising; ten to twenty gallons (45 to 90 litres) should cover most washing and cooking needs of a small family, with a little to spare. If the tank is too small it will mean endless stops to refill it; however, if the tank is too large it can affect the stability of the boat. Water weighs 10lb per gallon (4.5kg per 4.5 litres), and a large tank built without any internal baffles can allow the water to slosh from side to side, upsetting the trim of the boat. A pair of smaller tanks, one each side of the boat, coupled by a balance pipe will allow a decent capacity, without ruining the stability.

Water tanks need to be made from a corrosion-resistant material: high density polythene, butyl rubber and other plastics are the most suitable. Galvanized steel can be used, but it tends to fail after a few years and the rust will contaminate the water. Stainless steel is marvellous but the tanks can be difficult to fit.

Ideally the tanks should be fitted so that they can be removed from the boat for cleaning. It takes only a few years for a layer of debris to settle in the bottom, and this will soon start to fester; if the tank can be removed and given a really good shake and rinse out so much the better. Tanks can be sterilized with the same products that are used for cleaning babies' bottles. Water does go 'off' if stored for a long time – it becomes tainted with the taste of plastic, and harmful bacteria can grow in a stagnant tank, so it is worth cleaning it out at least once a year.

Flexible butyl rubber tanks are frequently used on cruisers. The nature of the boat means that there are odd-shaped spaces which will not accommodate a regular, rigid tank, and are wasted otherwise; a flexible tank will utilize these.

The tank's inlet pipe needs to be taken to a clearly marked filler cap, usually mounted on the gunwale. A wide-bore pipe fixed firmly to the deck fitting and the top of the tank will allow the air to escape as the water is poured in. A rigid tank will benefit from the addition of a separate vent pipe fixed at the far end of the tank and leading to a screened ventilator mounted higher than the filler. The pipes need to be attached rigidly to the tank with a stainless steel jubilee clip if they are the soft

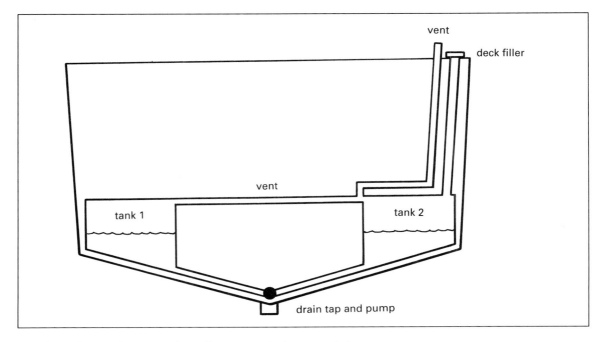

vent

deck filler

vent

tank 1

tank 2

drain tap and pump

A balanced pair of water tanks will increase the boat's stability.

plastic type. Screwed and compression fittings are unlikely to drop off. A stop-cock on the outlet of the tank will allow you to clean the filters or work on the system without having to drain out the whole tank.

Tanks need to be rigidly secured to the hull. A ten-gallon (45-litre) tank contains 100lb (45kg) of water, and in the event of a collision this could do serious damage to the boat if it came adrift. If the tanks are going to be removed for cleaning each year it is worth securing them with webbing straps anchored firmly to part of the hull. This will combine security with ease of maintenance.

Level gauges

Some kind of level gauge is a help. After all, it can be a bother tying up, unreeling the hose pipe and unlocking the tap, and it would be particularly annoying if it then transpired that you only needed a gallon in the tank. A clear pipe taken from the lowest point of the tank up to the top will make a very serviceable sight glass. It is also possible to get electrical sensors: float types usually screw into the top of the tank and work in much the same way as petrol gauges; electronic ones rely on a series of sensors mounted on a fixed dipstick, coupled to an electronic display. Although both types use only a minimal amount of electricity, over a period of time they will use up a noticeable proportion of the battery.

Pipework

The water system on a cruiser is not under high pressure and rarely becomes very hot, so ordinary food-grade plastic hose is suitable for the cold water, and a heavier duty version for the hot water system. Proper $\frac{5}{8}$in (15mm)

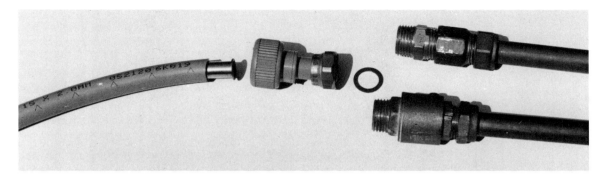

Copper and plastic pipes.

frost-proof domestic water pipes are excellent. Copper pipes are not suitable because they can be damaged by frost very easily. The pipes need to be secured to stop them rolling around and possibly bumping into the wires or gas pipes. A small boat with only a single sink will need ³⁄₈in (10mm) pipe diameter, and ⁵⁄₈in (15mm) will cope with the flow rates needed on all but the very largest cruisers.

Transparent pipe is used quite extensively on boats, but it does allow light to get to the water inside, thus providing ideal conditions for algae to grow. Since few people like green tea, it is worth making sure that the pipes are routed through dark areas; and strong sunlight on the pipe will not only encourage algal growth, it will also perish the plastic.

Filters

It is helpful to fit a couple of filters into the pipe between the tank and water pump. The first filter needs to be a coarse mesh type to trap particles of grit before they reach the pump, because this sort of contamination will wear out the valves and impeller. The second filter can be an activated charcoal filter which will take out any chemical contaminants. This will leave you with sparkling clear water from the tap. The coarse filter will probably need to have its wire mesh screen removed and washed about once a year; the charcoal filter will need to be replaced once it has done all the filtering it can. The water flow through it decreases and finally stops when this happens.

Water Pumps

Most cruisers normally have small, impeller-type pumps to move the water from tank to

A charcoal water filter.

A water pump with integral accumulator tank.

tap. These are usually reliable as long as the water going through them can be kept clean. They are sealed units and require little maintenance, although if they go wrong they can not normally be repaired. The pump does need to be connected to the electrical system by the correct thickness of wire. Larger boats need to be able to supply a couple of taps at once, say the galley and a shower simultaneously, and this will require a more powerful pump. Again the pump will require minimal maintenance, but it becomes more important to check that the pump is fed by the correct gauge wire since it draws more electricity.

Small plumbing systems are usually inert, and a switch mounted in the tap turns the pump on. This means that the pipes are never under pressure and are unlikely to work loose; however, it does mean that there is

quite a long stretch of wire between battery, switch and pump. This wire has a small but noticeable resistance, and if the wire looks a bit thin, check that the voltage across the pump's terminals doesn't drop more than 5 per cent below the battery voltage when it is operating; if it does, the wire is not adequate and needs replacing with heavier gauge. If a pump were used for a prolonged period with inadequate wire it would be damaged. The wire could also be a fire risk because it would be more likely to overheat.

Larger plumbing systems tend to be constantly pressurized. The water is compressed, and when the tap is opened a pressure switch in the pump housing detects the drop in pressure and switches the pump on automatically. When the tap is shut, the pressure rapidly builds up again and the switch turns the pump off. These systems are frequently fitted with an accumulator tank to even out the pressure switching. Like the smaller system, if the pump and switch are good quality and well installed there should be no need to do anything to them. These larger pumps also need to be checked for voltage drop when first installed. A guide to the correct wire sizes will be found in the chapter on electrical maintenance.

Sinks and Showers

Not much can go wrong with a sink or a shower basin. Nevertheless, it is important to check periodically that the seal around the edge is in good order; water trickling down the sides will set up wood rot in the fittings, so this eventuality needs to be avoided.

The waste pipe from the sink should be checked for secure fixing. It should be attached to the sink and hull outlet firmly so that the waste water doesn't accidentally end up in the bilges, and more importantly, so that water cannot get into the boat from outside. If the hull fitting is less than 10in (25cm) above the waterline the pipe must be secured

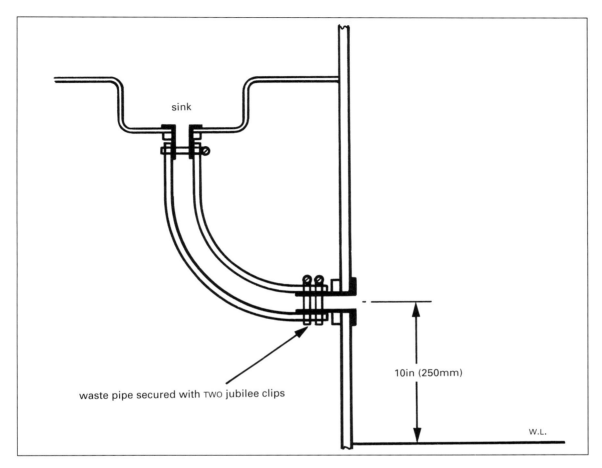

Sink drain and hull fitting.

with two jubilee clips and then be brought up to at least 10in (25cm) above the water internally; this is to prevent the boat being swamped in the event of a heavy list. The through-hull fitting needs to be examined at least once a year. On the inside it needs to be checked for tightness, and on the outside it has to be examined for signs of wear. It is all too easy for the outer face of the fitting to be worn away by contact with lock walls, and if that happens the remaining pipe will fall into the boat, letting the waste water into the bilges and possibly allowing river water into the hull.

Shower Drain Pumps

The waste from the shower tray has to be pumped overboard because the shower tray is so low in the boat. A diaphragm pump is the best type of pump for this application. Like the ordinary water pump, it is best to have a coarse filter and an adequate electrical supply. Impeller-type pumps have trouble dealing with the hair generally present in shower waste water; this wraps itself around the rotating impeller and causes it to seize up. Diaphragm pumps have no rotating parts in the housing, and so can cope better. The

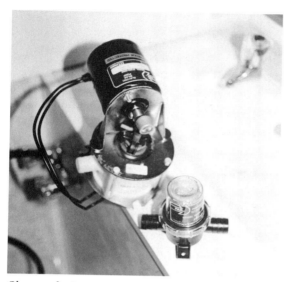

Shower drain pump.

coarse mesh filter will need a clean every now and then. The outlet needs to meet the same specification as the sink outlet.

Water Heating Systems

The restricted space on board an outboard motor driven cruiser creates some difficulties when it comes to providing a hot water system. Cruisers with inboard engines can utilize the excess heat of the engine to heat a calorifier; this is simply a tank with a coil in it warmed by the engine coolant. It is simple and straightforward to fit, and the heat is free. Outboard motors are not suitable for this, unfortunately.

Gas-fired Water Heaters

The most commonly fitted water heating system is the gas-fired instantaneous water heater; this uses LPG, and it heats water very effectively. The drawback is that to install one correctly involves meeting a great many

very strict regulations. In fact there are still a large number of appliances that are not correctly fitted, and these represent quite a serious threat because of their ability to release carbon monoxide into the cabin. They absolutely *must* be serviced once a year by a qualified and registered gas engineer. There will be a synopsis of the regulations in Chapter Seven, but the following few items should be checked straightaway.

Gas water heaters require a considerable volume of air and gas to burn cleanly. If the cabin does not have adequate ventilators, carbon monoxide will be produced by the flame. The heater will require at least $6in^2$ ($39cm^2$) of clear vent area in addition to its own flue, and in addition to any other ventilation needs. The manufacturers will supply a flue of a fixed length, and this should not be shortened under any circumstances. A lot of installations have been fitted with shortened

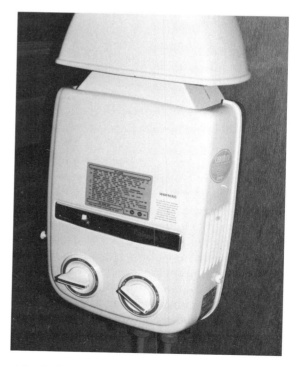

A typical gas water heater.

flues because of the restricted space in the boat, but this is *not* to be recommended because of the risk of exhaust fumes being blown back down the flue.

Gas water heaters generally use about 12cu.ft (3.4cu.m) of gas per hour, which requires a high volume regulator and a minimum size bottle of 13kg (28lb) for propane and 15kg (33lb) for butane. The bottle size is important because a small bottle can only evaporate a limited amount of gas from the liquid in it; a pressure drop can result if the off-take is greater than this limit. The gas pipe to the water heater must also be big enough to supply the correct amount of gas without causing a pressure drop; if the length of pipe is 10ft (3m) or less it should have a diameter of not less than $3/8$in (10mm), over this the pipe needs to be $1/2$in (12mm).

If your gas water heater does not meet these specifications, then call in a qualified gas fitter to sort it out for you.

Gas water heaters are particularly vulnerable to frost damage. The heat exchanger is made from light gauge metal which can be easily distorted and burst by water freezing inside it. It is therefore of the utmost importance that the heater is thoroughly drained out before the winter sets in.

Alternative Fuels

Manufacturers are now introducing diesel-fired water heaters and even cookers in an effort to phase out the use of LPG on boats. Even if your motor is petrol, a small tank of diesel is feasible to run the heating system. The boilers consume about a gallon of fuel a day, and will put out ample heat for that. Gravity-fed diesel boilers require a flue which will need to be swept clean once a year, or sooner if it gets blocked up; occasionally the filter will also need a clean, and the feed pipe into the burner may need a pipe cleaner run through it once in a while. Apart from this, they run quite happily for months on end.

Toilets

Most cruisers use the portable camping type of chemical toilet. These have the advantage that they can be stored in the shower tray out of the way, and they are normally free to empty. If your maintenance schedule includes a really thorough clean of the device every month, and also consistent use of the appropriate chemicals in both the flush and storage tanks, they shouldn't smell too bad.

Larger cruisers make use of fixed toilets with holding tanks for the waste. The tank has to be pumped out at a boatyard, and there is a fee to pay for this. Unlike a water tank this tank cannot be split into two with balance pipes, so it has to be sited centrally in the boat to avoid creating a list as it fills. It also needs to be secured to prevent movement during a bump. Maintenance for these toilets, apart from routine cleaning, is confined to flushing them through with a pint of warm water in which a tablespoon of cooking oil has been stirred. This will help prevent the rubber seals sticking, and is best done at the start and finish of each season. Toilets with macerator pumps are similar, but the pump may need to be disassembled to remove any blockages once in a while (utterly ghastly job).

Gas Systems

Gas aboard a boat is a tricky business these days: one look at the list of regulations is enough to convince most people that it would be easier to keep a badly house-trained tiger on the boat than a gas cooker. The trouble is that for the vast majority of cruisers, LPG is the only practical fuel for cooking and heating. Diesel is a fairly viable alternative in quite a lot of applications, but the cost of installation is sometimes greater than the value of the boat. Gas is cheap, versatile, and unfortunately explosive.

The latest batch of regulations has effectively

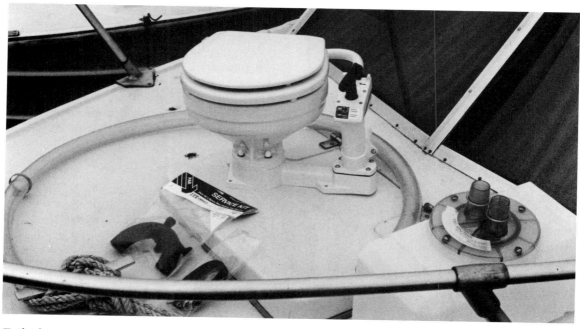

Toilet kit.

banned anyone working on gas appliances and systems unless qualified to do so. There is some argument about what the word 'competent' (as the law reads) means in relation to doing your own work, and it has generally been understood to mean 'qualified' i.e. having passed an examination to ascertain the quality and safety of the fitter's skill. This means that unless you have been registered as a gas fitter, you must not work on a gas system; in fact about all the unqualified operative can do is change the gas bottle and possibly even put the kettle on.

The reasons for these onerous restrictions are to be found in the long list of accidents involving LPG on boats. The gas is heavier than air, and so even a tiny leak will gradually fill the bilges of the boat with gas. Eventually the layer of gas meets a spark, and *Wallop!* . . . another statistic chalked up against gas systems. Carbon monoxide is another problem with gas systems: incomplete combustion of the gas generates this poisonous by-product, and quite a few people have dozed off to sleep, never to awaken. Faulty installation of even a simple gas system can result in either of these two circumstances.

There are several things that the boat owner can observe, which will help ensure that the system remains safe and has been installed correctly. Not all gas fitters are good at their job, even if they are qualified, and what is acceptable in a house is often nowhere near good enough for a marine installation. Let us consider these precautions.

Ventilation

The cabin is an enclosed space, and so it is essential that enough air can get in to replace the oxygen that a gas flame uses up. The alternative is to suffocate the occupants. People themselves don't use a large volume of

Good ventilation is the most crucial part of a gas system.

air, and only need about 1in² (6cm²) of vent each. Cookers are rather more greedy and need a great deal more; since they are not externally vented this air has to get into the boat, and the exhaust gases get out, through the vents. The need for air for combustion is most dramatically illustrated by the fact that a cubic foot of propane requires 23cu.ft of air to burn cleanly. If it doesn't get it, you have a serious problem.

The ventilation must be divided evenly between top vents and low vents. It is easy to overlook the lower ones, or even mistakenly to block them up because they let in cold air around your feet. Ventilator grills are prone to obstruction from cobwebs and dust, so it is very important to ensure that they are kept clean.

Ventilator Requirements

Per person: 1in² (6cm²)

Two-ring cooker with grill and oven: 30in² (193cm²)
Small catalytic heater: 8in² (52cm²)
Water heater, in addition to its flue: 6in² (39cm²)

These figures can be regarded as a minimum, and it would be worthwhile to organize some extra ventilation so that a crossflow of air can be achieved through the cabin space. This will serve to keep the air fresh and dry, and it will also mean that the fabrics inside stay wholesome for much longer.

Gas Demand and Cylinder Storage

Gas cylinders are bulky items to store on board. Furthermore they need to be kept in a position where any gas escaping will flow over the sides of the boat, and not into the bilges. Also, cylinders need to be of a big enough size for the gas inside to evaporate

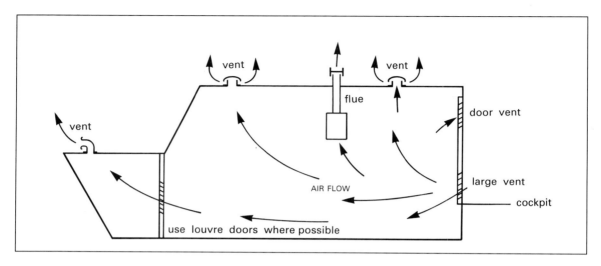

Typical cabin ventilation needs.

sufficiently quickly to replace that drawn off by the appliances they run.

These are the hourly consumption rates of some typical appliances:

Two-ring cooker with grill and oven

	8ft³ (0.25m³)
Simple two-ring cooker	4ft³ (0.15m³)
Instantaneous water heater	12ft³ (0.35m³)
Small fire	1.5ft³ (0.05m³)
Fridge	0.2ft³ (0.008m³)

The cylinders have to be able to supply the combined load of all the appliances on board. Their recommended hourly draw-off rates are as follows:

Butane

15kg	10ft³ (0.28m³)
7kg	7ft³ (0.2m³)
4.5kg	5ft³ (0.14m³)

Propane

19kg	25ft³ (0.7m³)
13kg	20ft³ (0.56m³)
3.9kg	10ft³ (0.28m³)

With these figures it is possible to calculate the minimum size cylinder you need to carry. For instance, if you have an instantaneous water heater, an oven cooker with two rings and a grill, a fridge and a small heater, the volume of gas the system might draw off the cylinder at peak rate will be in the region of 21.7ft³, and the smallest bottle that can supply that is a 19kg (42lb) propane cylinder. In practice it is most unlikely that anyone would ever want to use all the appliances simultaneously, so most boats get by with a 13kg (28lb) cylinder; but anything smaller is pushing your luck!

The cylinders themselves are normally kept in a gas locker, and this must have a vent from the bottom of the locker to the outside of the boat to let any spilt gas flow overboard. Often this is achieved by a pipe. However, the pipe is prone to blockage from cobwebs, and a bit of wire should be run through it every couple of months to dislodge them.

Regulators

The regulator needs to be in good condition and one of the non-adjustable types; one

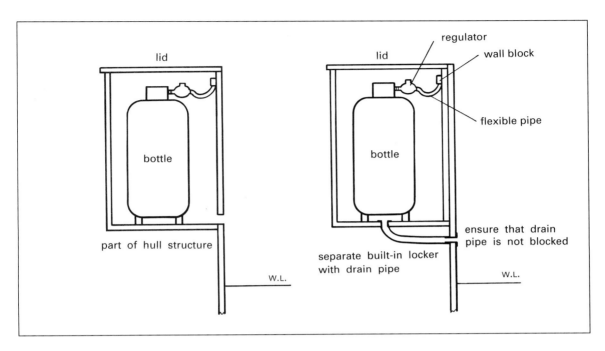

Gas locker.

scrounged off an oxy-acetylene pack will not do at all. The regulator also needs to be capable of passing the correct volume of gas. Virtually all regulators will manage the volumes required for a normal boat, with the possible exception of the small, clip-on butane regulator (182H) which passes about 15ft³ per hour (0.4m³).

Hose Tails

Inside the gas locker is the flexible section of the gas pipework, the pipe from the regulator to the wall block. It is most important that this pipe is suitable for LPG: the gas is quite chemically active and will eat away unsuitable material. The pipe needs to be inspected for wear and ageing each time the cylinder is changed, or once every month, whichever is sooner. Modern pipes are stamped with their year of manufacture, so you can see at a glance when they are getting old.

Pipes

The size of the pipe and the number of bends and connectors along it will determine how much the pressure drops when the gas is turned on. Old gas installations may not have been built to the latest standards, and it is wise to check whether yours are within modern specifications. The gas pipework should have an absolute minimum of bends and connectors. The pipes need to be supported by clips every foot (30cm) and within a couple of inches (5cm) of every connector. There should be no electrical wires within 6in (15cm) of the pipes, and preferably they should be a lot further away, like the other side of the boat. The pipes should not run in the bilges, and they should be protected from chafing where they pass through bulkheads.

Pipe diameters for appliances within 10ft (3m) of the cylinder
Two-ring grill and oven cooker: $^3/_8$in (10mm)
Instantaneous water heater: $^3/_8$in (10mm)
Small fire: ¼in (6mm)
Fridge: ¼in (6mm)

For pipe runs over 10ft (3m), the next size up pipe is advisable. If the pipework on your boat seems suspect, you should call in a registered engineer to rectify the problem.

Gas Appliances

Cookers, water heaters and non-catalytic fires all have an open flame which should burn with a clean, bright blue flame. Moreover the flame should be steady, and should not flicker when another appliance is turned on. If this is not the case, then an engineer should be called to sort out the problem. Cobwebs can cause trouble because spiders weave them in the open parts of the gas jets. The gas emerges from the nozzle to mix with the air in the tube leading to the gas ring; if there is a cobweb here the gas will emerge from the wrong end of the pipe and burn with a bright yellow flame. Turn it off immediately; the heat will not be enough to vaporize the cobweb, so it will be unable to rectify itself.

Each appliance needs to be serviced regularly in accordance with the manufacturers' instructions. Failure to keep to this schedule will not only invalidate the guarantee; it could invalidate you and your family, too.

Most LPG appliances will work on either propane or butane provided that it is at the correct pressure: butane equipment requires 28mbar, propane 37mbar. The regulator sets this pressure. If you are taking over an old boat it is always important to check that the appliances are suitable for the gas you intend to run them on. In fact, if you have just bought an old boat, treat the entire gas system as suspect until you have had it checked by a qualified fitter.

Leak Detection

There are two main ways to detect leaks in the gas system. The first is to use an electronic gas detector: this will be a constant drain on the battery since the unit consumes power all the time it is in operation, enough to flatten a battery in a week or so. Gas detectors are very effective and will alert you to any sudden leak as soon as it happens. Note that if the detector is wired directly to the battery, rather than through the boat's electrical system (via the main isolation switch), it must be provided with its own fuse.

The second method of leak detection is to place a pressure gauge between the regulator and the cylinder. These gauges are available from most chandlers and caravan shops and were originally designed to indicate the amount of fuel left in the cylinder, as well as to test for leaks. On the whole they are rather vague when it comes to checking the cylinder contents, but very good at showing the slightest leak in the system. Unbelievably, you are allowed to fit them yourself!

Summary

The fresh water stored on board a boat must remain in drinkable condition, and so the key element in maintaining the plumbing system is cleanliness. The system itself should require little routine work apart from an annual clean of the tanks, and changing or cleaning the filters as required. The quality of the installation will determine its reliability.

The gas system on board has to meet stringent standards these days, even if it is an old system. Although there is little practical work you can do to the system, it is very important to inspect it frequently so that no potential fault can turn into a dangerous situation. Gas has been one of the main causes of fatal accidents on the waterways, so it is in your own interests to meet all the safety rules.

— 5 —

Electrical Systems

The basic electrical system of a cruiser is a set of appliances connected via a fuse-board and isolation switch to a battery that is charged from an alternator on the motor. In practice things can get a bit more complicated than that, and like the other systems on board, the initial installation will determine the amount of maintenance and repairs it needs later.

What should be on a boat, and what there actually is on it, are frequently two different things. As boats get older they accumulate more equipment, and sometimes these extra bits get lashed into the system in a very haphazard way. If the wiring on your boat resembles a nasty accident in a spaghetti factory, then there is a good chance that the system is a fire risk. Although 12-volt systems pose no threat of electrocution, they can burst into flames just as easily as household wiring.

To prevent your boat incinerating itself, it is important that it meets the British Marine Electronics Associations Code of Practice. Copies of this code are available from the British Marine Industries Federation. Wiring needs to be installed to a professional standard to avoid any hazards, and in fact it isn't difficult to do this.

Electrical Generation

The alternator on an inboard engine is capable of producing a current of about 20 amps when the motor is running above tick-over. This will provide more than enough power to run all the equipment you are likely to want to use. Outboard motors produce substantially less power, older models are likely to have a charging rate of only 2 amps and newer ones about 5 amps. Therefore if the outboard motor is running for six hours a day it will produce at best a total charge of thirty amp-hours. If your electrical consumption is above this, some other means will need to be found to augment the supply.

Power Demand Calculations

Each appliance draws so much current, and operates for so long; for instance a radio will draw about 1 amp and probably be on for three hours a day, thus it will use three amp-hours; a water pump will draw 4 amps but only be on for ¼ hour, thus using one amp-hour. From these figures it is possible to calculate roughly the daily demand in amp-hours and then compare that to the power available from the motor.

Appliance	Current +	Likely hours' use
Water pump	4	¼ – ½
Radio	1	2 – 3
Television (small)	3	? as much as you like
Fluorescent light	1	3 – 4
Shower pump	4	¼ – ½
Navigation lights	10	1 average
Bilge pump	3	never, hopefully
Fridge	6 – 8	24
Gas detector	1	24
Burglar alarm (PIR)	1	24

If the total you expect to use exceeds about thirty amp-hours for an outboard motor, or 120 for an inboard, then additional power generation will be required. Appliances that are on continuously soon push up the total, and are best avoided if possible.

Sources of Energy

Solar Panels

Silicon solar arrays can produce worthwhile quantities of extra power during the summer. They are easy to mount on the roof and are maintenance free, and they should last over ten years, too, all of which makes them ideal for cruisers. Their power output is dependent on their size: a square metre of them will put out about eighty amp-hours on a good sunny day. They are also of use in the winter, when they can keep the batteries fully charged even if the boat is left tied up for months. Batteries like to be kept in a fully charged condition (more of that later).

Wind Generators

Like solar panels, wind generators can also enhance the power available, but are of limited use whilst cruising because they need to be on top of a mast to catch the wind, and so have to be dropped down to avoid bridges. Small wind generators produce a maximum charge of about thirty amp-hours a day in summer, and 300+ in winter storms; it depends on the weather.

Both the sun and the wind provide free and environmentally clean power, but the relevant systems do cost a bit to install. Moreover their performance is dependent on the climate; since this can involve long periods of charge, they both need a voltage regulator to avoid over-charging the batteries.

Stand-by Generators

Small petrol generators, either 12- or 240-volt types, need to be treated with some care on a boat. The problem arises from leakage of petrol vapour from the carburettor and when filling their tanks. They can provide a great deal of electricity, but need to be used and stored with due regard to all the regulations pertaining to petrol (and there are plenty).

Batteries

The power, from whatever source, is stored in the batteries. Motors that have an electric start facility need a battery dedicated solely to themselves, and a separate battery to run the rest of the equipment. This is to prevent a prolonged stop flattening the battery so much that the engine cannot be restarted. Electric start motors usually have a manual start facility, but they are so awkward to use that it makes sense not to have to try!

Manual start motors are connected to the battery via a flying lead; sometimes this needs to incorporate a diode if the motor generates alternating current. Most put out direct current these days. A fuse rated slightly above the maximum charging current should be fitted in the lead.

Types of Battery

The battery for the engine needs to be an ordinary cranking type; these are designed to deal with the high currents demanded by the starter motor. Electric start outboards don't normally need a massive battery to turn them over; the engine's manual will suggest the ideal size.

The cabin battery is normally a deep cycle or leisure type because these can stand a prolonged, although smaller current drain, much better. The repeated charge/discharge cycle that the cabin battery is put through places a

Built-in diesel generator.

greater strain on the plates, and they need to be made of stronger lead alloy.

Care of Batteries

All lead acid batteries detest being discharged totally, and to keep them in good condition it is best to keep them as fully charged as possible all the time. This is particularly relevant during the winter when the boat is not used regularly. If the battery is going to be left for any longer than a month, it will need a top-up charge to keep it fresh.

The electrolyte level in the battery needs to be checked every month, and if the level has dropped it should be topped up with distilled water. The ideal level is ¼in (6mm) above the top of the plates. Sealed batteries have to live without topping up, and so it is important that they are charged properly. Fast charging is the cause of battery 'gassing' and loss of electrolyte. Most outboards and inboard alternators do not produce enough power to overcharge a battery, but if charging up the battery at home, never try to rush the job or it will harm the battery.

The batteries need to be firmly secured to the hull so that they don't get knocked over when the boat bumps into a lock. The best way to achieve this is to have them strapped into a compartment on their own. Battery boxes are useful for this since they usually contain the all-important cover to prevent accidental short-circuits when you drop a spanner across the terminals. The box has to be secured, too.

The batteries need to be ventilated overboard. During the charging cycle hydrogen and oxygen are released in an explosive mixture, and it is important that these gases can escape. Any switches mounted within the battery compartment must therefore be 'ignition protected' so that a stray spark doesn't ignite these gases.

The battery terminals suffer from corrosion quite badly because they are so close to the acid. Once the terminals have been bolted on to a clean terminal, they need a liberal coat of heavy grease to prevent the corrosion. Once a year these terminals will need a good clean and a polish with emery paper to brighten them up.

Determining the Battery Size Required

How big should the cabin battery be? This can be calculated from the daily demand. For example, if you use thirty amp-hours each day, then the utterly minimum size of battery would be thirty amp-hours. However, since this would involve completely flattening the battery and recharging it every day, the poor thing would soon be fit only for the scrap-heap: thus a sixty amp-hour battery would be the practical minimum because it would never be more than half discharged — although a ninety amp-hour would be even better since it is well in excess of the minimum, and will not cost that much more than a sixty amp-hour one. Also if you can limit the power used to about 10 – 30 per cent of the available capacity, it will greatly extend the life of the battery. Note that if cranking grade batteries are used, as opposed to deep cycle ones, it is particularly important to avoid flattening them.

Isolation Switch

Between the batteries and the circuit there must be a heavy duty switch to isolate the system; this is important in the event of an electrical fire caused by a short-circuit. You might be able to extinguish the fire with an extinguisher, but if the short is still merrily sparking away it will only re-ignite; operating the switch will stop this happening. Electric motor start systems using two batteries

The isolation switch must be clearly marked.

normally have the switch placed in the common negative of the batteries; single battery systems can have the switch in either the positive or negative lead of the battery. This way the switch will cut off all electricity from every circuit. Burglar alarms, gas detectors and automatic bilge pumps can bypass the switch only if they have their own individual fuses. The switch will normally need to be able to take a 100-amp load, unless the boat has an inboard engine when 150 amps will be required. Switches with a removable key are quite handy since they will prevent intruders being able to turn on the power readily.

Split Charging Systems

When two batteries are fitted, one for the motor and one for the cabin equipment, some form of charge control is essential. This can be achieved by switching the cabin battery into the cranking battery charging circuit only when the alternator is producing power, and switching it out of the engine's circuit

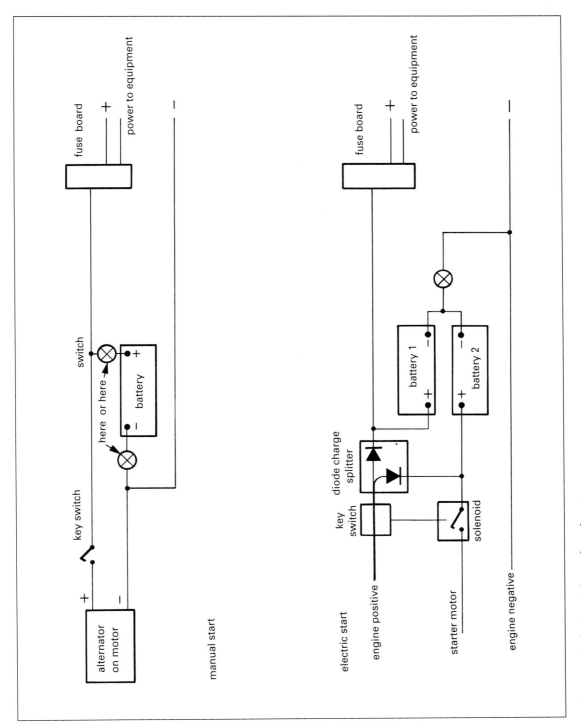

Isolation switch circuit for outboard motors.

Electronic charge controller.

when it is not running. This effectively keeps the cranking battery constantly at peak charge. There are several ways to do this.

Manual switching with a large four-way switch is simple and reliable. The switch has four settings: 'Off', 'Batt 1', 'Batt 2' and 'Both'. Select 'Batt 1' for engine starting and perhaps an hour of charging afterwards, then 'Both' for the rest of the day. When the motor is turned off and you are in the cabin, select 'Batt 2', and when the boat is unattended, turn them all off.

Diode Charge Splitters

Electricity can only flow in one direction through a diode, and these splitters utilize this property to let the power from the alternator flow through a pair of diodes to the pair of batteries. Since the power can't flow back through the diode, it can't get from the full to the flat battery. The catch is that diodes cause a voltage drop across them of about ¾ volt, which prevents the batteries becoming 100

per cent charged. Newer, more sophisticated charge splitters don't suffer from this problem – but of course they cost more!

Split Charge Relays

A relay that automatically connects the two batteries together only when the engine is charging is a very handy device. It allows the full voltage to get to the batteries, like the manual switch, and it does it automatically like the diodes. It seems to offer the best of both worlds, apart from one little catch: since the unit appears to be a 'fit and forget' gadget, everyone does just that. However, in practice it is important to check it once a year to make sure that the fuse in the feed to the cabin battery hasn't blown, and this fuse is the first thing to check if the cabin battery doesn't appear to be taking a charge any more. The fuse rating is normally 15 amps; if the cabin battery has become deeply discharged whilst the cranking battery remains at its right charge, when the relay is activated a huge

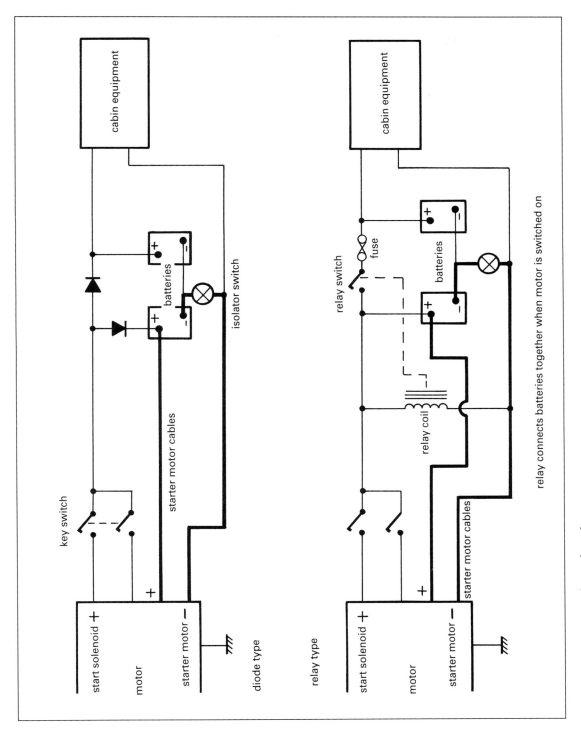

Split-charging systems for outboard motors.

current will try to cross from the one to the other, and blow the fuse.

Most relays are designed for the caravan market. They have a pair of wires feeding the coil, one going to a point in the engine's electrical circuit that is only on when the engine is on (such as the positive just after the ignition key), and the other going to the negative. The other pair of wires is the bridge between the batteries. Some relays have an additional parallel terminal for another appliance, such as a fridge. Very few electrical devices designed for cars and caravans are ignition protected, and it is best to treat them with care; for instance, never mount them in proximity to battery gases or petrol vapour.

Fuse- and Distribution Boards

There is a wide variety of fuse-boards and distribution panels available. The main aim of them is to provide a safe connection point for the wires serving the appliances, together with a clear array of switches and fuses. The board needs to be mounted somewhere dry and that is easy to get at, particularly if the switches are mounted on the same board. Because all boats have to be wired with a twin conductor system – they do not use the chassis as a return in the way cars do – the board will need to have a connector built in to accommodate all the negative wires as well as the positive ones. Small automotive fuse-boards don't often have this facility, and a strip of connector block lashed into the back of the board is not really good enough.

Different types of fuse-board.

demand of the appliance, but slightly below that of the wire serving it; for instance, a water pump that draws 5 amps would require a 6-amp fuse but be wired with cable capable of taking 10 amps; in this way if a short-circuit occurs in the pump, the fuse will blow long before the wire overheats. Quite a lot of boats are using miniature circuit-breakers mounted in household consumer units these days, and the systems are neat and tidy even if they are not exactly marine grade. Don't forget that an amp remains an amp whether it is in a 240-volt AC or a 12-volt DC system, and it is the power that is affected by the difference, not the current.

Fuses

Fuses are designed and put in to protect the whole system from fire if a short-circuit occurs, so they are rather important. Each appliance must have its own fuse. The fuse should be rated slightly above the current

Wires

Boats shake about a fair bit, and so ordinary, single-core household wire is not suitable: it will gradually harden and become brittle, then it cracks, and then it fails. During the process it first reduces the voltage available to the appliance, then it creates dreadful radio interference as it starts to spark inside the insulation, and then it sets the boat on fire; so all in all, it is a liability.

Good quality, automotive grade wire is essential for marine use. It comes in a variety of colours so the circuits can be colour-coded, and a selection of thicknesses so that the appliances can draw their correct power from the battery. All the wiring in the boat will need to be inspected once a year to check that it is still in good condition. The wires should always remain flexible, they should be the correct colour – fading or browning may indicate that the wire is over-heating – and the insulation should not be chafed or holed. The terminals need to be inspected to make sure that they are not working loose or corroding.

Cable Sizes

Copper wire has a small, but noticeable resistance to electricity. On a high voltage system this has little practical effect, but on a 12-volt system it has to be taken into account. The longer the wire the greater the resistance, and thus the greater the loss of power. Conversely the fatter the wire, the lower the resistance. It is very much like a water pipe, and plumbing terms are frequently used to explain electrical actions (though they don't help much for computers!).

The effect of wire resistance means that each appliance has to be wired with a cable that is just fat enough to deliver all the power it needs: too fat is needlessly expensive, and too thin is likely to overheat. To select the right wire is a matter of working out the length of the wire run, and the current it must carry, and matching that to a chart to see what is the best wire. You can, of course, work out the resistance per metre yourself, but it isn't really necessary.

Current (amps)	5	10	15	20
Distance (metres)				
5 (16ft)	1	1.5	3	4.5
10 (32ft)	2.5	4	5	8
15 (48ft)	3	5	6	10
20 (65ft)	6	8	10	15

Wire cross-section in mm2

The distance is the complete length of the wire, from battery to appliance and back again. The current is the maximum that the device will require; this is usually written on it, but if the power is known it can be calculated thus: amps = power (watts) divided by the voltage. For example, a 50-watt headlamp running at 12 volts is 50/12 = 4.16 amps, which we can call 5 to be generous, and if that is, say, five metres (16ft) from the battery – which means ten metres (32ft) of wire – it will need to be wired up with 1.5mm^2 wire, and to be on the safe side it is best to choose the next size up which is 2.5mm^2. Simple enough maths, basic physics coupled with typical engineering over specification; ask any engineer what two and two are, and he will usually say eight to be on the safe side.

The wires need to be physically supported so that they don't stretch under their own weight. This can be with wire clips, which are notoriously difficult to nail into GRP boats, or in a proper cable duct screwed to the hull. Either way the wires must be kept well clear of gas and fuel pipes, and run as high as practicable.

Appliances

Appliances on board can range from a couple of lights and a water pump, right up to a floating disco with washing machines and microwaves. Most cruisers, however, simply do not have the space for fiendishly complicated electrical appliances, nor do they have the power generation capacity to run them, either. It is best to use the engineer's maxim 'Keep It Simple'. Wherever possible use low energy lighting to conserve the available power, and use all lights economically; this is better than having to buy a generator!

Some equipment, such as a car radio, has its chassis connected to one of the power leads; thus a negative earth radio will have its box connected to the negative wire, and a positive earth radio will have its box connected to the positive wire. Because the hull of the boat is not a conductor (unless you have a steel boat) this doesn't make a huge amount of difference; nevertheless, it is a good policy to stick to one polarity to avoid accidentally shorting the system by touching the case of one against the case of another. Most modern automotive equipment is negative earth, so it makes sense to use that polarity.

Internal Lighting

Fluorescent Lights

These lights are very energy-efficient, but many are designed for the caravan market and are therefore not particularly well suited to the humid environment of a boat. They consist of a little inverter to generate the high voltage required to light the tube. This voltage can deliver a shock if the terminals are touched, so be careful. The tubes last a long time, but when they start to discolour at the ends it is worth replacing them. The inverter makes a high-pitched whine, which can interfere with radios; it may need a suppressor across the power terminals. The switches in these units are the usual point to fail because of corrosion on the terminals. For those who know about these things then they are easy enough to clean up; but if you are no good at electronics, then find someone who is, because there is no point in paying for a

new one when the problem can be solved with a bit of emery paper. A single 12in (30cm) fluorescent tube will draw about 1 amp, a double one about 2 amps.

Filament Lights

Filament lights are much less efficient since they generate heat as well as light, although personally I prefer to sacrifice some efficiency for their much more homely colour, and I know I am not alone in this. The current draw of the lights can be calculated by dividing the power (watts) by the voltage (12, in this case).

Pumps

The pumps on board are the most power-hungry appliances; for example, a water or shower drain pump will normally require a supply of 5 to 10 amps, and so it is important to select the correct size wire to serve them. The terminals on water pumps are often exposed to damp air, so it is worth checking once a year that they are not corroding. A bit of grease, or better still, fully shrouded terminals will prevent this problem.

Navigation Lights

As most cruising is a day-time occupation it is easy to overlook these lights, until the boat starts to burrow into a tunnel, and then it is really a bit late. It is worth checking that they work before starting a cruise.

Other Equipment

There is a whole host of gadgets that can be fitted onto a cruiser: depth sounders, radar, televisions and even mobile phones (assuming that your cruise is not specifically to avoid these). However, no matter how fancy a gadget, the basic power economy of the generating system has to be respected, and you can't use more power than you generate

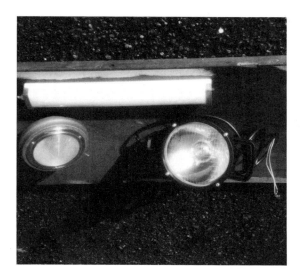

Fluorescent and filament lights.

240 Volts and Inverters

It can be a real help to have a 240 volt AC power supply aboard. Power tools, hoovers, microwaves and irons all require a mains supply, and all of these can be very useful on board. Inverters are electronic gadgets that convert the power stored in the battery to 240 volts AC. Nevertheless, the power economy principle still holds true, unfortunately, and if a 500-watt load is drawn from the inverter it will flatten the batteries in a very short time indeed. This is not too bad a problem for boats with an inboard engine, but it could leave an outboard driven power system in the dark.

Care is needed, however, because 240 volts, whether it is from an inverter or a plug at home, is quite capable of killing. Most inverters are fitted with overload sensors as standard and are intrinsically safe, but that is no reason to treat it any less carefully. All 240-volt systems must meet BMEA Codes of Practice, even though there is no requirement stated in the new Boat Safety Scheme to do this. However, just because they haven't

on board. There are so many devices available that it would be impossible to catalogue them all and list their maintenance needs; the appropriate manufacturer's handbook will have all that information.

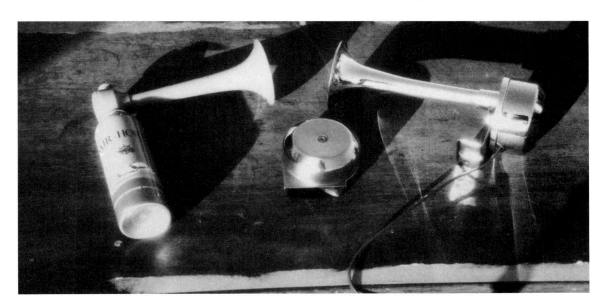

Air and electric horns; pick the loudest!

Inverters need to be carefully installed.

dreamt up a regulation to cover something doesn't mean that you can be any less careful.

Inverters can draw massive currents from the batteries, and the battery bank will need to be upgraded to cater for this. Fifty amp-hours per 100 watts is a pretty good basis, although you can get away with less; as with the ordinary power storage, the less the batteries are stressed, the longer they will last. The wire connecting the battery to the inverter needs to be very thick stuff: a 100-watt inverter will draw about 10 amps, which isn't too bad, but a 1,000-watt one will draw 100 amps and will require 25mm² cable if it is only one metre (3ft) from the batteries.

Summary

The maintenance of a well installed electrical system is simply a matter of examining it closely once a year for damage, and keeping an eye on the electrolyte levels in the batteries. If the system hasn't been well made it is quite likely to be a fire risk, and should be replaced at the earliest opportunity. Although 12-volt systems don't appear dangerous, they can and do cause fires if they fail badly, so the maintenance of the system is important. Those who are not confident of being able to install or alter the system in accordance with the BMEA Code of Practice, should not attempt to do so. Nobody wants to see a boat go up in flames.

— 6 —

Internal Fittings and Furniture

The interior of a cruiser is an object lesson in squeezing a quart into a pint pot. The basic rules of physics seem to defy the notion that it is possible to have reasonable accommodation in a cruiser, and yet boat builders have managed to find a way somehow. A well fitted cruiser does provide comfort, warmth and a reasonable level of facilities within its small space, but this is extremely dependent on everything working correctly. If the bed or table doesn't slide in or out properly, if the lights fail or if everything starts to smell musty and damp, then the boat soon ceases to be an attractive venue for your holidays.

Condensation has to be the bane of boats, forming on all the cold metal or plastic

Steel cruisers have a bit more room.

surfaces as the warm, moisture-laden air comes in contact with them. My old boat was so bad that I used to dread waking up in the mornings because I knew that the moment I moved, the drops on the ceiling above my head would descend, splat. Luckily there are ways to reduce the problem, good ventilation being at the top of the list.

Ventilation

An adequate supply of air is not only important to supply the heaters with oxygen, it serves as a drier, too. Moisture in the air will very quickly damage the fabrics and woodwork inside the boat, and the condensation will wreak havoc: books and papers become soggy, and black spots of mildew appear all over the place; regardless of the size of boat, if there isn't a free movement of air through the cabin, including through the cupboards, it will not be long before moulds and wood rots start to grow. Most boats are fitted with very little ventilation even when they come directly from the manufacturers; this shows after a few years, and in the worst cases dry rot may be starting to eat up all the wood.

Moisture enters the boat through several routes. The easiest to put right are those leaky windows and canopies, as these can be traced and mended, but some sources simply cannot be cured – the boat's occupants can't stop breathing, and it is unlikely that they will stop cooking, either. The average person will release a couple of pints of moisture a day in

Ventilation is vital, or the boat goes rotten.

his or her breath, so the only solution is to remove this humid air by good ventilation.

There is a price to pay, however, for the removal of the humid air through numerous vents, this being that the boat will need to have a greater heat input to keep it warm. If the heaters are open flame gas burners, they will also be releasing moisture, so there is a limit to what can be achieved. Heaters that expel their exhaust gases through a flue are ideal, providing a dry heat that will keep the boat smelling fresh as well as being warm.

Natural Draught Ventilation

There are two ways of ensuring a good flow of air through the boat: a natural draught which works without any power, and forced draught using extractor fans and bilge blowers. The latter requires power, and thus is only capable of working when the boat is in use; the long periods when it is laid up tend to allow the stagnant air to damage the fittings.

Ventilators need to be positioned both in

Various types of ventilator.

the roof and as low as possible to achieve an upward flow of the air. This allows warm, moist air to exit at the top of the cabin, to be replaced with cool dry air at the bottom. Theoretically the split between the two should be 50/50. Although the figures provided for ventilating the gas appliances will meet the regulations (*see* Chapter 4), to keep the boat properly vented it is worth doubling those figures. Opening windows does provide plenty of air, but it is often just when you need the most air movement – say, a slightly chilly autumn evening – that you will want them closed, so fixed vents are the best. Careful positioning should eliminate any awkward draughts.

Cupboards can become particularly stale and stagnant, especially those in the galley and bathroom, so it is worth placing vents or louvres in the doors; this will keep the air fresh, and also provide plenty of easy routes for spiders which just love living on warm dry boats. A good movement of air will reduce the chances of wood rots quite dramatically.

A word of warning: ventilators are often fitted with flyscreens to keep out mosquitos, and these soon become blocked up by nature's own flyscreens, cobwebs. It is a good idea to clean the screens once a year to ensure that the air can still move freely through them; apart from that, there is no main-tenance needed.

Forced Draught Ventilation

Forced draught ventilation is a bit more com-plicated. **Extractor fans** and **cooker hoods** are very useful at removing cooking smells, but they soon get covered in grease and dust. Most cooker hoods have some sort of filter to catch the worst of the grease, and this will need a wash-out every so often. A lot of these hoods also have a small fluorescent light mounted in them, which also gets coated with grease. The tube can be removed and

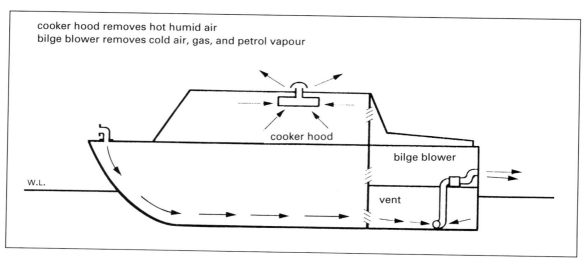

cooker hood removes hot humid air
bilge blower removes cold air, gas, and petrol vapour

cooker hood

bilge blower

vent

W.L.

Forced draught ventilation.

Don't forget to air the shower compartment.

cleaned, but remember that these lights have a small inverter generating a high voltage, so to avoid an unexpected jolt make sure that the unit is isolated from the power system before tinkering with it. The tube needs to be really dry before replacing it.

Bilge blowers are particularly valuable on petrol-powered boats because they suck out the air, complete with petrol and LPG vapour, from the lowest point where they collect, and blow them over the side. However, bilge blowers *must* be ignition-protected because of this: there wouldn't be much point in sucking out the gases only to ignite them. The maintenance of these units is very simple, merely to keep them clean. Using the blower regularly will reduce the risk of accidental ignition of petrol vapour, and will keep the bilges smelling very much fresher.

Woodwork

Most of the internal furniture and also the bulkheads are made of wood, a lightweight, strong and versatile material, but prone to

A bilge blower.

damage from water. Solid tropical hard-woods such as mahogany and marine-grade plywoods are the usual woods used because of their longevity. Softwoods such as pine and internal grades of ply are not suitable, although there are quite a few boats with them in. Composite sheets such as chipboard are a waste of space, but they still crop up from time to time, usually because they have to be replaced. Good ventilation will reduce the humidity inside, and thus keep the wood in better condition.

Wood Rots

Wood rots are best kept at bay by water-proofing the superstructure and ensuring that the cabins are dry. However, if either wet or dry rot does start to grow, it is important to cure it, and to stop the cause of the damp which will have caused the rot.

Dry Rot

Dry rot is a scourge of boats; it flourishes in damp conditions, despite its name, and can be difficult to eradicate. The symptoms are easy to spot once you are familiar with it: the first sign is a distinctly musty fungal smell, long before there is anything visible to see, and in time this is followed by a fine web of microscopic white filaments growing along the wood. The wood starts to change its appearance, first looking slightly damper, and then becoming brittle and apparently dry, breaking up into cube-like sections. The last stage is when the fungus forms its fruit-ing body, which is a large mat of dense growth, brown with a white border; it rather

It's worth keeping the wood looking good.

resembles a science fiction invader from space, and does just as much damage: if things have got this bad, you have a major rebuilding project on your hands.

Dry rot is fairly rare on inland boats, but if it does occur the cure has to be dramatic. All the infected wood, and all the apparently sound wood within a yard of the edge of the outbreak, has to be removed; this is because the microscopic filaments travel long distances and need to be removed to prevent further infection. The whole structure of the boat then needs to be treated with a powerful anti-fungal agent, and the new wood will also need to be treated before it goes back in. All this sounds rather drastic, and if what appears to be dry rot starts growing in your boat, get in a specialist to identify it with certainty before going ahead and demolishing the cabin!

Wet Rot

Wet rot can do nearly as much damage to the wood but is simpler to identify and cure. It is caused by constant exposure to water, particularly sources such as dripping windows or poorly drained decks. The wood gradually becomes soft and spongy, holding an increasing amount of water in its fabric, and eventually is so soft that you can put your finger through it. If the bit happens to be a structural timber, the whole fabric of the boat can be threatened.

Wet rot is not so invasive as dry rot, and does not require the same draconian measures. The affected wood will need to be cut back to sound timber – and this must be *really* sound timber, otherwise it will start up again – and fresh timber treated with preservative can be spliced into place. The leaky window, or whatever it is, must be identified and waterproofed to prevent a recurrence.

Cutting out Rot

Cutting away large chunks of a boat's timbers and bulkheads needs a bit of planning. Every timber or sheet of plywood has a purpose, usually holding something else up, so if you just whip out a bit of timber without any forethought at all, something else is likely to fall off as a result. Check where the timbers are secured, and what other elements of the structure are supported by them. The usual sites of wood rots are along the floor, which often means that whole seats or cupboards will need to come out to get at the rotten part.

Where a piece of wood needs to be removed, it helps to try and get it out in one piece so that it can form a template for its replacement. The new piece will need to be fixed in place with a good strong fixing, either screws, bolts or adhesive. Screws and bolts are best made from a non-corrosive metal such as brass or stainless steel; ordinary steel with rust away before your eyes. There are several very strong glues on the market which are waterproof, and also have a reasonable filler content so they will stick to rough surfaces if needs be. Where wood has to be bonded to the GRP surface, a web of new fibreglass and matting can be formed to make a very secure mounting.

Fibreglass resin bonds to wood very well as long as the wood is clean and dry; if, however, it has been treated with a preservative it is important to allow the solvents to dry off completely or they will prevent a good bond forming.

On the whole it is best to keep the boat well aired to reduce the chances of an outbreak of rot, than to have to sort out the mess afterwards.

Care of Wood

The woodwork of doors and cabin furniture will need a fresh coat of varnish every few years: done properly, this will make the interior look like new. The action of sunlight, water and ageing gradually spoils the appearance of varnish, making it cloudy and spoiling the gloss shine, and if the varnish becomes seriously worn this process will start to affect the wood behind it, making it fade unevenly.

If you have had the boat from new, you will be able to recognize when a fresh coat of varnish is desirable, long before the wood starts to fade. To renew this finish is a bit of a performance, but worth all the effort. First, everything that can be moved out of the cabin should be moved out, as the second stage of the proceedings will generate dust in magnificent proportions. Once the cabin is clear, all the wood should be sanded lightly with a fine sandpaper. If the wood and the existing varnish are in good condition it isn't vital to get back to bare wood, only to achieve an even surface that will take a new coat. Once the sanding is complete, the dust has to be removed, which is easier said than done. An industrial vacuum cleaner with an exhaust pipe is the best tool, because it will blow the exhaust air down the pipe and out of the boat. When all the dust has settled, then it is a matter of applying a fresh coat of varnish.

Yacht varnishes are the best, although modern polyurethane ones are pretty good. Non-boaters have this belief that there is some mystic and arcane secret behind varnishing, thinking that yacht varnish has to be the best varnish possible. What they fail to realize is that boat woodwork is usually looked after a lot better than their shelves, and that really, a varnished surface is only as good as the person who looks after it.

Decks

The wooden cockpit floor on most cruisers

Mouldy fabrics ruin a boat.

takes an awful pounding. It gets wet, usually because it starts to rain when you get to a lock, and then it gets muddy. If the boat has an inboard engine then it is probably cooked as well. The rest of the time there is probably a little leak in the canopy keeping one corner constantly damp. All this does not amount to the perfect conditions for longevity.

The best wood for this floor is a high grade marine plywood; ordinary external grade will not last nearly as long. The best way to ensure that it does last is to keep the leaks from the canopy to a minimum (it would be marvellous to say stop them altogether, but canopies are not like that) and to keep the space beneath them well ventilated. Non-slip surfaces on the top are a great help when it comes to practicalities, and an aluminium edge around the corners also helps keep them tidy. The underside can either be painted with floor paint, or better still treated with a semi-porous wood stain which will allow the wood to breathe.

If the old floor is crumbling under the strain, lift up the boards and use them as templates for new ones while you still can. The bearers beneath the floor need to be kept as clean as possible; corners where the dirt can accumulate will soon become damp and start to rot.

Fabrics

There are plenty of curtains and cushions aboard a boat, and the first and most important element in their maintenance is to ensure that they are properly flame-retardant. This is not always the case, and most boat mattresses, for example, are made of plastic foam, which can be extremely dangerous in the event of a fire.

Household furniture has to meet stringent flame-retardant tests nowadays, and this is also a requirement of boat furniture, as laid down by the Boat Safety Scheme: in short, it should be able to pass the match test. Many boats have cushions dating back long before these rules were introduced, and because the foam is expensive, it tends not to be replaced but only to have new covers put over it. If you are not sure whether the foam inside the mattresses or cushions in your boat is flame-retardant, it is worth testing it, a straightforward operation. Remove a small sample, say a one-inch cube, from inside where the hole won't make any difference, and take it outside and hold a lit match against it. If it catches fire rather than melts into a sticky mess, then it is not flame-retardant, and it will need to be replaced.

The curtains and seat covers also need to be flame-retardant. Dralon is the most commonly used material, and this is normally treated in manufacture to resist fire. If the seat covers have got so grubby that they need a clean, a dry cleaners can undertake to keep the flame-retardant quality if you ask them. Curtains usually need more washing, but can be treated with a spray-on flame-retardant after they have dried.

Carpets also pose a fire risk. Older types with wool and hessian materials in them are very low risk, but modern synthetic materials are about as dangerous as foams. They can give off huge quantities of toxic smoke and can burn very readily, and it is certainly worth testing them. Carpet forms a very comfortable wall-lining for cruisers, insulating the boat and reducing condensation, although it is not that suitable for ceilings because of its weight (it drops off) and because of the fire risk.

Fittings and Furniture

Because a boat is subject to vibration and knocks, the equipment in the cabin needs to be mounted strongly. A cooker weighs a fair bit, and each time the boat bumps against a lock wall it is shaken; in the course of time this can loosen the mounting bolts, or even the cupboard to which it is bolted. The same holds true for other things such as water heaters, and even the radio. Each piece needs to be examined at least once a year to see that it is still firmly mounted, and to make sure that the pipes or wires are not coming loose.

Gas pipes and electrical wiring have had increasingly stringent regulations imposed on them to reduce the risks of fire and explosion. Older boats are to some extent exempt, but this doesn't mean to say that a potentially dangerous situation can be left untouched until it actually blows. Gas pipes, for example, may need to be secured more rigidly, and if that is the case a CORGI registered fitter will need to be called in. The electrical wiring may also need attention in an older boat. The BMEA Code of Practice gives a detailed description of what is currently considered to be the best way of doing things, its main purport being that the wiring should be contained within a duct so that it is both easily accessible and protected from contact with anything else. These ducts can be added into an existing boat by bolting or screwing them along the corner of the ceiling, which is the best location, or along the underside of the gunwales, which is a good second-best. There is a range of ducting available these days, not just the white plastic box section, but moulding made to look like wood (not that many trees grow square branches with clip-on lids!).

Much of the furniture on board is fixed to the structure and needs to be well maintained because replacement is a complicated business. Door hinges and bolts need regular oiling to keep them freely moving, and drawers will benefit from a smear of candle wax or beeswax along their runners to keep their action smooth. Caring for the wood has already been discussed.

Insects

People are not the only species keen on boating: there seem to be a host of creepy crawlies that like to come aboard, too, and since they don't offer to help with the mooring fees, most people want rid of them. Spiders are the quickest on board. A dry boat is very attractive to them, and although they do help to reduce the fly population they are a nuisance when they build their webs over the vents and windows. A well sealed boat keeps most of them at bay, but otherwise it is a matter of personally evicting the rest of them.

Woodlice and silverfish often appear in older boats, and they are a symptom of damp wood; both eat the wood as it goes soft, so if you find the little monsters it is worth examining those dark corners thoroughly to find the spot where the wood is going soft before the boat requires a major refit. If they are a problem there is an insecticidal spray which can be applied to the surfaces that they walk over, and this poisons them; it is also effective against ants. Food stored in anything other than glass screw-top jars will encourage all sorts of bugs on board, too.

A winter lay-up provides a great opportunity for all sorts of creatures to hibernate on board. Butterflies and lacewings don't usually upset people, but creatures such as mink can cause havoc on board, dragging their fish meals into the cabin and never doing the

washing up! It is worth taking the effort to ensure that there aren't any gaps big enough for them to gain entrance.

Annual Checks

Inspect all woodwork for signs of damp or rot.

When the soft furnishings are cleaned, make sure that their flame-retardant properties are kept.

Lubricate all hinges, bolts and drawer runners.

Inspect the varnished surfaces to identify the best time to revarnish them.

Clean and test all ventilators.

Check that all appliances are secured properly.

Summary

Maintaining the interior of the boat is one part ventilation and two parts cleanliness. If the boat is always clean, then odd patches of damp or rot will be immediately obvious, and thus attended to straightaway. Every few years another coat of varnish will keep the boat looking like new, if not better.

The Boat Safety Scheme

In 1980 the first attempt by the British Waterways Board to enforce reasonable standards of boat construction and maintenance was put in place. It was designed to ensure that hire boats and residential craft attained some very basic minimum safety standards. Several people had been killed in accidents resulting from poor design or workmanship on a boat, and a number of fires had resulted in further deaths, and the Board felt it was essential to reduce these risks as far as possible. At the time they suggested that the scheme would eventually encompass all private boats, too.

In 1990 they tried to implement the original Grey Book set of standards. These transpired to be too stringent for many existing boats and there was an uproar, so the

Virtually all powered boats need a certificate.

scheme was withdrawn for reconsideration. Whilst all this was going on the mandarins of Brussels were trying to agree on a set of common standards for recreational craft so there would be no barriers to trade within the EU. Thus the revised Boat Safety Scheme was also going to have to include and conform to the Directive on Recreational Craft; all of which was supposed to have been completed by the celebrated 1992 free trade date. In fact the whole plan is more or less six years behind schedule, although it is still roughly on the same tracks. The new Boat Safety Scheme contains much less retrospective regulation so that existing boats, as long as they are still largely within their original specification, will be granted their certificate.

The EU directive is the superior legislation in all this snowstorm of paper, and the Safety Scheme has been drawn up to reflect this, particularly Annex 1. Our government has to make the directive law by 16 December 1995, and it will start to be implemented from 16 June the following year, with a two year period of adjustment. Sensible boatbuilders are already putting the directive into practice; most are simply hoping that the whole thing will just go away: it won't.

New boats for the inland waterways will be boat design category D, able to withstand a wind force up to and including force 4 (Beaufort Scale) and waves up to and including 0.5 metres high. The boats will have to meet various standards laid out in Annex 1, and have good handling characteristics. Every new boat will have a hull identification number, and also the manufacturer's code, country of manufacture, serial number, year of production and model year. The boat will also have a builders' plate fixed to it stating the manufacturer's name, CE marking, boat design category, maximum recommended load and the number of persons the boat is designed for; there will even be an owner's manual. Annex 1 of the Safety Scheme is therefore quite thorough, since it has had

hundreds of people beavering away in committee rooms for nearly a decade. One does just wonder how much it has all cost to produce. In detail the scheme is as follows.

Part 1

Part 1 refers to the scope of the scheme, the sorts of boats covered by it, and the exemptions for maintenance craft. Unless you have a coastal boat using inland waterways for a transit crossing through Scotland, you will be expected to comply with all the others. Historic and existing boats are allowed certain exemptions. Part 2 is a list of the required specifications; there will only be a comment on the clause where it seems worthwhile.

Part 2

2.1 *Filling pipes shall be taken to deck level, or so arranged as to ensure that any fuel overflowing will not be discharged into any part of the vessel including the bilges.*
Many of the clauses, such as this one, are simple and straightforward both to implement and to understand why they have been drawn up. It is worth remembering that the standards were drawn up by a committee that had to take into account all sorts of different craft, from a little Shetland to a Thames barge.
2.2 *The filling pipe shall have an internal diameter of at least 38mm (1½in), and any flexible hose shall be of non-kinking material suitable for the fuel used, and must be connected with leak-proof joints between the top of the tank and a screwcap or plate forming the filling connection. All flexible hoses shall be adequately supported and of minimum practicable length, with all joints or connections readily accessible.*
Existing boats with a 1¼in (31mm) filling pipe do not need to make any alterations.

Petrol is explosive! Great care must therefore be taken, hence all the rules.

2.3 *All deck and fuel filling connections shall be situated so as to minimize the risk of cross contamination and shall be clearly marked on the deck fittings or immediately beside them indicating the purpose of each connection and, in the case of fuel connections, the exact type of fuel.*

2.4 *A vent pipe of minimum practicable length with an internal diameter of not less than 12mm (½in) shall be fitted at the highest point of every fuel tank and connected with leak proof joints. The material used shall be non-kinking and approved for use with the fuel concerned.*

Existing boats with a vent pipe of ³⁄₈in (9mm) are acceptable, and boats without a vent can install one in the filler cap as long as it has the flame arrester specified in the next clause.

2.5 *A vent pipe shall extend to a height equal to or greater than that of the deck filling connection, and the open end of a vent pipe shall be fitted in a position where no danger will be incurred from escaping fuel or vapour. Each opening shall be furnished with an effective wire gauze diaphragm flame arrester of non-corrosive material. The flame arrester shall be fitted with a gauze of mesh not less than 11 to the linear centimetre (28 to the linear inch), and the total area of the clear openings shall not be less than the cross-sectional area of the air pipe.*

2.6 *Fuel tanks shall be properly secured, and be installed as low as practicable, and be constructed of a suitable non-corrosive material. Materials used in the construction of fuel tanks shall have a minimum fire resistance of*

30 mins in accordance with BS476 part 20. Tanks shall have sustained a pressure test of 0.25 kgf/cm² (3.5lbf/in²) before installation and be marked to indicate this. All joints and seams shall be efficiently welded, brazed or close riveted to sustain a pressure test of 0.25 kgf/cm² (3.5lbf/in²).

Boats with inboard engines will need to be sure that if they have GRP tanks, the tanks are made with a fire-resistant grade of GRP. Some grades of aluminium are acceptable, namely 5052, 5083, 5086 and 5454; however, ordinary aluminium is not strong enough.

2.7 *No petrol or paraffin tank of more than 2.5 litres (½ gallon) shall be installed within 1 metre (39½in) of any engine or heating appliance unless it is insulated and protected by an efficient baffle of fire-resistant material.*

There is no actual figure relating to quite what the efficient baffle of fire-resistant material is, so you and your surveyor will need to use a bit of common sense; thus if the material of the baffle meets BS 476 part 20, and it effectively shields the tank, there should not be any problems.

2.8 *Glass or plastic fuel sight gauges shall not be used. Fuel level indicators, if fitted, shall be of a type which does not allow escape of fuel or vapour in the event of damage to the indicator. Dipsticks when fitted shall be calibrated and only be used via gas-tight fittings. Where a dipstick is used, it must be made so that it cannot strike the bottom of the tank.*

This is a simple enough clause: old commercial boats are exempt from it, but that is all.

2.9 *Tanks shall be accessible and all connections shall be readily accessible for inspection.*

This is particularly important on some makes of cruiser where the fuel filler pipes are prone to falling off.

2.10 *Tanks shall be effectively bonded by low resistance metallic conductors of adequate strength to their deck filling connections, and in the case of a non-conducting deck or hull,*

tanks shall also be electrically bonded to an earth point in direct electrical contact with the surrounding water, for the discharge of static electricity.

The BMEA Code of Practice has details of earthing a boat so that static electricity and even lightning strikes can be earthed without the whole lot going up in flames. A good earth to a point where the electricity can get through the hull into the water is very important, particularly where static can build up on the boat, and spark across to a petrol pump nozzle . . . boom!

2.11 *Tanks may be drained only by means of a suitable drain valve fitted with a plug on the outlet.*

2.12 *The fuel supply shall be drawn through the top of the tank or as near to the top of the tank as is practicable by means of an internal pipe extending to near the bottom of the tank. In the case only of gravity feed systems a feed from a cock or valve directly screwed in near the bottom of the tank is permitted. Any return fuel line required to be connected to the fuel tank shall be connected through the top of the tank or as near to the top of the tank as is practicable.*

2.13 *All fuel feeds and pipes permanently charged with fuel shall be made of softened copper, stainless steel, aluminium alloy or (for diesel installations only) mild steel of suitable size, fixed clear of exhaust systems and heating apparatus and adequately supported to minimize vibration and strain. Any balance pipe between fuel tanks must comply with the requirements of this standard and must in addition be fitted with valves directly attached to the tank and so constructed that they will not become slack when the valves are operated.*

It is most important to comply with this clause, as suspect pipework is one of the principal causes of fires.

2.14 *Flexible tubing may only be used in the engine compartment and shall be suitable for the fuel used. It shall be of minimum* *practicable length, be reinforced, and have an internal diameter of not more than half its external diameter, and have a fire-resisting quality as required by BS MA 102.*

There are two new numbers to watch for: pipe meeting ISO 7840 is acceptable, and so is DIN 4798. This latter one is very new, a steel-braided, flexible pipe which has three orange stripes incorporated into the braid. It is actually well in excess of the minimum fire safety needs.

2.15 *All connections shall be made with efficient screwed, compression, cone, brazed or flanged joints. Soft-soldered joints shall not be used.*

Soft solder does not like vibration, and it will suffer from metal fatigue on a boat.

2.16 *All fuel filters shall be suitable for marine use and shall be of fire-resistant quality.*

This means that filters must meet the fire-resistance standard used above.

2.17 *A cock or valve shall be fitted in the fuel feed pipe as near as possible to the fuel tank in a position where it is readily accessible. If it is not visible the position shall be clearly marked. In all petrol engine installations where the steering position is remote from the fuel tank a second cock or means of operating the main cock or valve to close the tank shall be fitted, immediately accessible from the steering position.*

Boats that have both a centre cockpit and an outboard engine are almost certainly going to need the accessory kit from their engine manufacturer to meet this standard. Most ordinary cruisers have the helm so close to the motor and tank that this is not a problem.

2.18 *Fuel pipes shall not be run in the bilge water areas.*

Of course not . . . What a ghastly place to be situated!

2.19 *Carburettors (other than of the down draught type) shall be fitted so as to allow any overflow therefrom to drain into a spirit-tight metal drip-tray, the top of which shall be covered with copper or brass gauze of flame-arresting mesh soldered to the tray all round. The tray shall be removable or be fitted with a cock for emptying. A flame trap or air filter must be fitted to the air intake of petrol, petroil, and paraffin engines.*

A complicated but essential clause: it is surprising how many back fires set the carb ablaze, and then the rest of the boat.

2.20 *The engine shall be securely installed.*

This may appear to be stating the obvious, but poor installation accounts for over 80 per cent of breakdowns requiring work under the engine's warranty.

2.21 *Every vessel shall have effective means of reversing operable from the steering position. The engine stop control shall be located as near to the steering position as practicable.*

The word 'practicable' occurs quite often in these clauses. In this case it means 'taking all reasonable steps to bring the stop control close to the steerer's position'; if it was going to cost a fortune to do this for the last yard (or metre), then that last yard would be deemed impracticable, and the boat could still get its certificate. On some old outboards it may not be feasible to cut up the engine wiring to provide a remote stop switch without jeopardizing the safe running of the motor, and that would be considered impracticable: put simply, the risks of adapting the engine to meet the clause would be greater than the risks of leaving it alone.

2.22 *An oil-tight tray made of metal or other suitable material, the sides of which must be carried up as high as practical, shall be fitted beneath every engine and gearbox so as to prevent leakage of oil escaping into any part of the vessel or overboard. A tray is not required if oil-tight structural members are fitted fore and aft of the engine. No fixed bilge pump is to draw from the oil-tight area.*

Outboard motors automatically meet this clause. Inboards should have a special tray already fitted. 'As high as practical' means

4in (100mm) if possible, and if less, then as high as can possibly be fitted in the space available.

2.23 *The cylinders and exhaust system shall be effectively cooled and shall allow for the dissipation of heat. In the case of air cooled engines or where water is not passed through the exhaust system, the exhaust pipe shall be effectively lagged or shielded.*

Outboards already have the appropriate heat insulation. Inboards will need insulation from just after the manifold (which is impractical to wrap) to the point at which the water from the cooling system cools the exhaust gases, or the hull outlet. To meet the spirit as well as the letter of this clause, it is best to angle the exhaust blast down towards the water rather than horizontally where it will foul other boats and lock sides.

2.24 *Exhaust noise shall be effectively suppressed, and no form of exhaust silencer cut-out shall be used.*

Clauses **2.25** and **2.26** refer to steam- and LPG-powered engine installations. Steam or LPG engines have to meet all sorts of regulations, and there just isn't room here to go into them all. The appropriate user group will be able to advise.

Part 3

Part 3 of the Safety Scheme refers to electrical installation; the specifications are as follows:

3.1 *All batteries shall be securely installed so as to prevent movement and damage. All battery compartments shall be adequately ventilated and covered with insulating and non-corrosive material. No battery may be fitted beneath or adjacent to any petrol or LPG tank, cylinder, cock, pipe or filter.*

There is a lot of power stored in a battery and it is easy to forget just how much of a punch it can deliver . . . until you drop a spanner

Electrical systems can get complicated.

across the terminals. Batteries are also very heavy, and if the boat bumps into a lock and they are not properly secured, they will quite happily continue on a forward path, breaking anything in their way. As mentioned earlier, the explosive gases released on charging must be well ventilated.

3.2 *Cables shall be of adequate current-carrying capacity and of suitable construction and grade. They shall be insulated and/or sheathed so as to be impervious to attack by fuel or water. They shall be adequately supported, or run in adequately supported suitable conduit.*

The BMEA Code of Practice goes into thorough detail, and any boat wired in accordance with that will have no problems meeting all these specifications.

3.3 *Main circuits shall be installed above bilge water level and all except starter circuits* *shall be protected by circuit breakers or fuses of the appropriate rating and of a suitable design.*

3.4 *All cables shall be installed as high as practicable in the vessel, and they shall be run clear of all sources of heat such as exhaust pipes. They shall not be run adjacent to fuel or gas pipes unless contained in suitable conduit. PVC insulated and/or sheathed cables shall not be run in direct contact with polystyrene insulation.*

3.5 *A master battery switch capable of disconnecting the system (including the starter circuits) shall be installed in a readily accessible position as close to the battery as possible. The battery master switch must be capable of carrying the maximum current of the system. Electric bilge pumps, security alarms and fire pumps when fitted may have circuits which by-pass the master switch, but only if separately protected by fuses.*

Boats with outboard motors will not require a massive master switch; one of the little ones with a red key will be quite adequate. Boats with inboard engines may well require a heavier duty switch, especially diesel engines.

3.6 *Main starter-motor leads subject to high current shall have soldered or pressure-crimped connectors. Spark-plug leads shall be supported clear of the engine block and cylinder head.*

Even though there is a clear safety element to this clause, it is also essential for reliable running of the motor; the electrical connections have enough to contend with anyway, because of the high humidity, and loose connections would be the final straw.

3.7 *All electrical devices fitted in any compartment containing petrol or gas shall be ignition-protected in accordance with BS 7489.*

This is now BSEN 28846, but the principle is still just as important: that it only takes a spark to turn your boat into a Viking funeral.

3.8 *All electrical equipment shall be two-wire*

insulated except in respect of the engine circuits where there must be a low-resistance return conductor between the battery and the engine. Engine installations with two-wire insulated electrical systems do not require fitting of the low-resistance return conductor.

3.9 *The spark ignition and generating systems of engines and all electrical equipment on the vessel shall be effectively suppressed against causing radio and television interference.*

Part 4

Part 4 of the Boat Safety Scheme relates to electrically propelled boats, and since there is only a tiny number of boats with electric power plants, the space available does not justify a detailed examination of this section. In years to come electric boats will become more popular, much as they were at the turn of the century. New specifications for charging points are being drawn up, and one day someone will invent a better battery which will make the idea much more feasible. At present, electrically powered boats are more or less in the same category as steam- and gas-powered ones, an important minority; however wonderful they are (and they are), they are severely handicapped by the pathetic capacity of modern batteries.

Part 5

Part 5 relates to outboard and portable engines, and is of immense interest to most cruiser owners. In principle, all motors will comply if they are in their original condition, with fuel lines and tanks as supplied or approved by the manufacturer. If the motor, fuel pipes or tanks, or electrical connections are not what the manufacturer fitted, then the installation is suspect.

Even the most clearly marked deck fillers must be kept clean to be legible.

5.1 *All deck and fuel filling connections shall be situated so as to minimize the risk of cross contamination, and shall be clearly marked on the deck fittings or immediately beside them indicating the purpose of each connection, and in the case of fuel connections the exact type of fuel.*

One would hope that this will prevent diesel getting into a petrol tank or petrol into the water tank. Some idiot is bound to get it wrong if it isn't clearly labelled.

5.2 *Permanently installed fuel systems shall comply with Standards 2.1 to 2.19 inclusive, and they and all associated pipework, cocks etc shall be suitably protected against external impact.*

This is relevant to inboard engines more than outboards. The standards are fairly precise about the minimum requirements of the fuel system, and the need to prevent pipes from accidental damage is quite important. When the EU legislation is in place, there will be an ISO number specifying the exact detail which new boats will have to meet.

5.3 *Portable fuel tanks carried inboard and connected by flexible piping to the engine carburettor, and close-coupled fuel tanks forming an integral part of the engine may be used, providing that the fuel supply can be readily shut off and no unauthorized modifications are made to the equipment as supplied by the manufacturers. Portable fuel tanks shall be clearly marked with the type of fuel to be used, and when not in use shall be stowed in accordance with standards 7.2 and 7.3.*

This standard means *no jerry cans*. The fuel system for an outboard motor or generator must meet the manufacturer's specifications, and a haphazard arrangement of old tins is not acceptable at all. Portable fuel tanks need their own vented locker of the same type as the gas locker, so that any petrol vapour can get out of the boat. This does mean two vented lockers, one for petrol and another for gas. Hanging the petrol tank or gas cylinder in a frame over the back of the boat is not a solution, since they are then vulnerable to impact.

5.4 *Petrol not carried in fuel tanks shall be stowed in containers conforming with the requirements of the Petroleum Spirit (Motor Vehicles, &c) Regulations 1929 (SR &O 1929/952) or the Petroleum Spirit (Plastic Containers) regulations S.I. 1982 No 630 and these shall be stowed in accordance with Standard 7.2 and 7.3.*

This is another kick in the teeth for the 4-gallon (18-litre) jerry can (in fact they are only designed for diesel). The normal interpretation of the petroleum spirit regulations is that a maximum of two 1-gallon (5-litre) containers, meeting the specification, can be carried in addition to the outboard's fuel tank.

5.5 relates to engines powered by LPG, and as far as I know there are not any cruisers of this design. If you have one, it must comply with the LPGITA Code of Practice specification No 18.

5.6 to 5.8 effectively duplicate other standards. 5.8 again stresses the importance of

storing LPG and engines and fuel tanks in lockers which will vent gas and fuel vapour overboard. Also that petrol and gas should never be stored in the same locker; it might sound like a nuisance to store them in a separate locker outside, but this really *is* a life-saving regulation.

Part 6

Part 6 is concerned with fire prevention and fire extinguishing equipment.

6.1 *Powered vessels or vessels carrying or fitted with cooking, heating, refrigerating or lighting appliances shall be equipped with not less than the number of portable extinguishers detailed below, which shall be of a type approved by the BSI and/or British Approvals of Fire Equipment scheme. Extinguishers shall be kept in readily accessible positions adjacent to fire-risk points, and shall be properly maintained in good condition for immediate use. Any portable extinguisher provided for the protection of an engine space shall be capable of being discharged without fully opening the primary access.*

The number of extinguishers may be reduced by one fire extinguisher with a fire rating of no more than 5A/34b where either:

(a) no cooking, heating, refrigerating, lighting or fuel-burning appliances are carried;

Length of vessel	Minimum number of extinguishers	Minimum fire rating of each extinguisher	Minimum combined fire rating of extinguishers
up to 7m	2	5A/34B	10A/68B
7m–11m	2	5A/34B	13A/89B
over 11m	3	5A/34B	21A/144B

(b) no engine is installed.

A nice, straightforward clause: now everyone can rush out and buy great numbers of extinguishers of the right type. And even the numbers given here are a definite minimum, because these small extinguishers will fight a fire for only a few seconds: if it is not under control by then, get the boat to the side and get off. If you have a safe opportunity – and only if – it is worth throwing the gas cylinders and spare petrol cans overboard; the fire brigade are not keen to go too close to burning boats when the gas cylinders are still aboard, and who can blame them! Remember that in the event of a fire your insurance policy can get you another shiny new boat, but no one will be able to replace your friends and relatives: so concentrate on saving people first. The best policy is to take all possible steps to avoid a fire in the first place.

6.2 *Any fixed system installed for the protection of a fire risk space shall be in addition to the portable extinguishers required by Standard 6.1, and if remotely operated the release device shall be readily accessible from outside that space.*

If you have a fire in the engine bay it is crucial that you do *not* lift up the covers to fire an extinguisher into the space: you will be met with a faceful of flames. Remotely operated extinguishers are perfect for this application, otherwise an ordinary extinguisher needs to be shot into the space through any suitable aperture; air vents should be the best.

Areas exposed to heat must be heat resistant.

6.3 *In vessels fitted with cooking facilities, a fire blanket marked as complying with the 'Light Duty' requirements of BS 6575 and ready for immediate use, shall be kept nearby.*

Have you got one at home?

6.4 *In vessels with hulls constructed of glass-fibre reinforced plastic (GRP) those areas of high fire risk, such as an engine room or fuel compartment, shall have any exposed GRP structure coated with suitable fire-retardant material complying with the Class 2 requirements of BS 476: Part 7.*

Existing boats do not have to meet this standard; however, it is worth examining a boat to make sure that it is not likely to catch fire too easily.

6.5 *Polystyrene thermal insulation shall comply with the Type A requirements of BS 3837: Part 1.*

There is not much call for this insulation in cruisers. However, it is worth noting that thin grades of polystyrene have occasionally been used as a wallpaper to help reduce condensation. If you have this material in your cabin it is wise to be sure that it is flame-retardant by pulling a bit off and applying a match to it – outside the boat, of course! Existing boats are exempt from this clause, but it is worth complying with anyway.

6.6 *All soft furnishings, fabrics and foam materials used in the lining out and furnishing of vessels shall be of suitable fire-resistant materials, which on combustion release minimal amounts of toxic products. Upholstery fabrics used shall satisfy the cigarette and butane flame tests of BS 5852: Part 1.*

Again, existing boats are exempt from this clause too, but it is worth bearing in mind when you are planning to change the furnishings. Non-fire-retardant foams are positively lethal if they catch fire, so do you really want them on your boat?

6.7 *All vessels shall have two means of escape from accommodation areas. All means of escape shall have a minimum clear opening*

of 0.2m² (310in²) and a minimum width of 380mm (15in).

Existing vessels are expected to meet this clause where it is possible to do so without incurring major structural alterations to the boat. Some smaller boats cannot be fitted with a second exit, but since they are so small you are virtually sitting in the doorway anyway, so this is not considered to be a problem. In short, if it is possible to comply, do so; if it is not, don't worry.

Part 7

Part 7 is concerned with LPG (Liquefied Petroleum Gas) installations, and this is where the specifications get really tough! All those accidents associated with LPG have had causes, and this whole section is designed to reduce these causes to a minimum. The standards are fairly self-explanatory, often referring to other laws and codes of practice which are very detailed indeed. Your registered CORGI gas fitter is the one to blame if anything goes wrong now; he should know all about all the regulations.

Existing installations that have been passed by a surveyor should be left alone, apart from regular servicing by a qualified engineer. It is important that the systems are kept in optimum condition.

7.1 *The installation shall comply with BS 5482:"Domestic Butane and Propane Gas Burning Installations, Part 3: Installations in Boats, Yachts and other Vessels", except that:*

(a) the pressure drop of 2.5 mbar specified in Appendix C may be exceeded if, when all burners are lit, the flames are steady and of the correct proportions;

(b) open flue spillage tests as required by Clause 4.3.2. of BS 5440, Part 1 need not be conducted if the ventilation arrangements fully comply with the requirements of BS 5482, Part 3;

(c) the pipe sizes recommended in BS 5482, Part 3 are to be regarded as for guidance only.

7.2 *Every container (whether in use or not) shall be either: (i) secured on an open deck away from hatches and other openings so that any escaping gas is dispersed overboard; or (ii) secured in a separate compartment or box above the waterline, with gas-proof and flame-retarding sides and bottom, and with a lid or cover. Such a compartment or box shall be of sufficient depth to contain the height of the cylinder(s), cylinder valve(s), and regulator(s). Such a compartment or box shall have provision for allowing any escaping gas to be vented overboard by means of a metal or flexible pipe suitable for use with LPG, or a direct opening through the side of the vessel as near as is practicable to the bottom of the compartment or box. The lower pipe or opening shall have a minimum internal diameter of 12mm (½in) for a cylinder of up to 15kg capacity, and shall be enlarged in cross-sectional area proportionately for additional gas storage.*

7.3 *Any compartment or box as specified under Standard 7.2 (ii) shall be constructed of sheet metal of 0.9mm (20 w.g.) minimum thickness with joints welded or brazed, or of fire-retarding glass-fibre reinforced plastic of adequate thickness. The materials used in the construction of a locker or compartment shall have a fire resistance of 30 min in accordance with BS 476, Part 20.*

There is an exemption for existing boats, but like most of these exemptions, if you have the chance to bring the boat up to the new standard, so much the better.

7.4 *All containers shall be installed in an upright position with the valve uppermost and not adjacent to any cooking or heating appliance, or in an engine or fuel or battery compartment.*

7.5 *Ready access to the main gas valve(s) shall be provided at all times. If the main gas valve(s) are not visible their position(s) shall be clearly marked.*

7.6 *Pressure regulators may be mounted either separately from the cylinder(s) or with a direct connection to the cylinder(s). Pressure regulators not directly connected to cylinders shall be securely fixed and suitably protected within the compartment specified in Standard 7.2 (ii). In both cases a flexible connection to BS 3212 Type 2 shall be fitted to facilitate the replacement of cylinders. Pressure regulators of the external manual-adjustment type shall not be fitted.*

7.7 *Each point intended for use with a portable appliance shall be provided with a readily accessible control tap and bayonet or screwed connection.*

7.8 *Where self-contained portable gas appliances having the burner screwed direct to the container are used, such appliances, if stored in the vessel, shall be placed in a compartment or locker constructed in accordance with Standard 7.2 (ii). Self-contained portable gas appliances shall not be used whilst unattended on board any vessel.*

This means camping stoves and blow torches. They are not often found on cruisers, but if you have one, keep it in the gas locker.

7.9 *Flexible tubing conforming to BS 3212 Type 2 of minimum practicable length and fitted with integral threaded metallic ends shall be used:*

(i) for the immediate connections to containers or to regulators directly attached thereto but not extended to the interior of the vessel or outside a vented container housing; and

(ii) for the connections between portable appliances and their control points.

The 'integral threaded metallic ends' bit has recently been deleted. Any Calor Gas stockist will be able to advise on suitable flexible piping.

7.10 *All fixed pipework other than that which forms an integral part of gas-burning appliances shall be made of solid drawn copper or stainless steel.*

7.11 *All fixed pipework shall be as short and*

run as high as practicable and shall be rigidly secured. It shall be adequately protected against mechanical damage and deterioration.

7.12 *No pipework shall be run through the bilge-water area or adjacent to electric cables (unless the cables are contained in suitable conduit – see Standard 3.4) or adjacent to exhaust pipes or in any other position prejudicial to its safety.*

It shall not be run through petrol engine compartments and/or compartments specifically designed to contain or containing electrical equipment including batteries, unless carried in gasproof conduit admitting jointless pipe only.

7.13 *Joints in pipework shall be kept to a minimum, and they shall be readily accessible for inspection. Joints shall be made with compression fittings and rigidly secured. (Note: when gas is not being used it is advisable to turn off the valve on the container. Where two containers are connected to a manifold or tee, both container valves should be closed before either container is disconnected. Any spare or empty containers on board must either be on deck or in the ventilated housing.*

7.14 *An approved gas test point shall be fitted at the furthest practicable point from the supply. (Note: an approved bubble tester is highly recommended in order that boat owners may easily check for gas leaks. Such a tester shall be securely fixed in the gas-tight compartment or box as defined by Standards 7.2 and 7.3).*

The gas test point can be fitted by a Calor Gas or CORGI registered fitter. It is also possible to buy a pressure gauge which fits between the regulator and cylinder which will indicate any leaks. Since minor leaks are hard to detect simply by smelling for gas, these testers can provide valuable early warning of a problem.

Part 8

Part 8 is concerned with appliances.

8.1 *All fuel installations for cooking, heating, refrigerating and lighting appliances shall be installed in accordance with the appropriate parts of these Standards.*

8.2 *The pilot lights and/or burners on all gas or paraffin refrigerators installed in petrol-engined vessels shall be completely enclosed. Air for combustion must be:*
(i) drawn and exhausted through an approved flame trap, or
(ii) piped to the appliance from outside the vessel or from a point inside the vessel above the level of the ports, windows or other means of ventilation in the compartment in which the appliance is installed.

It will not be long before EU regulations insist that all pilot light appliances are the 'room-sealed, balanced-flue' type. At present it is virtually impossible to get a gas-powered fridge to comply with these standards on a petrol-powered boat. Electrically operated fridges are the best alternative, even though they consume a fair bit of power. The only other option is to go shopping for fresh food every day; very nostalgic.

8.3 *All LPG or fuel oil appliances of the catalytic type or with pilot lights or having continuously burning flames shall incorporate a flame failure device to cut off the gas or fuel supply to the main and pilot burners. Catalytic appliances shall also comply in all respects with the requirements of BS 5258, Part 11.*

8.4 *Appliances fired by fuel oil shall have a valve or cock to shut off the supply in a readily accessible position within the same compartment as, but at a safe distance from, the appliances.*

8.5 *Woodwork and all other combustible materials including curtains adjacent to all appliances shall be suitably insulated and protected against excessive heat, or be* inherently flame-retardant, or be treated with a durable flame-retardant.

8.6 All permanently installed domestic cooking, heating, lighting or refrigerating appliances shall be secured in order to eliminate undue strain on pipework or fittings and to prevent overturning in the event of a collision, and shall be properly installed.

8.7 Oil-fired or LPG appliances shall not be installed in the engine space in petrol-engined vessels.

8.8 Every fuel-burning appliance which requires a flue and, where fitted, a draught diverter shall be of an approved type and properly fitted and maintained. The flue shall be of adequate internal diameter, effectively insulated and of suitable material to ensure safe passage of gases to the outside of the vessel.

8.9 The water inlet to any water heater shall be piped only from the boat's cold water system.

8.10 Adequate ventilation of a type which cannot be shut off shall be provided in accordance with the requirements of BS 5482, Part 3 in vessels in which LPG or liquid fuel appliances are used. (Note: ventilators should be weathertight to cater for the worst conditions likely to be encountered by the vessel.)

Part 9

Part 9 deals with pollution.

No sanitation system capable of discharging sewage overboard shall be fitted in any vessel unless it is capable of being sealed or rendered inoperable. Sanitation systems shall comply with the requirements of BS MA 101. We will be hearing more about this section as pollution controls become ever more strict. At present, 'grey water' – the waste from showers and sinks – is permitted to be drained overboard; however, this practice may yet be banned, and it will have to go into a holding tank.

Pump-outs may one day be compulsory for washing-up water, too.

Part 10

Part 10 is all about hire boats and new boats, which don't really concern us here; though Annex A has new standards for new boats to comply with the EU directive.

Annex A

When the revised Boat Safety Scheme was launched in 1992 this annex was left rather vague, principally because it would be superseded by the standards introduced by the Directive for Recreational Craft. The directive covers all recreational craft, so quite a lot of it is not much help on the sheltered waters of the UK. These new standards are for boats built once the directive is in force. The new Annex A has just been published, and this is what it looks like (serious Eurospeak):

1 Boat Design Categories

Inland cruisers are in category D, 'Sheltered Waters':

Designed for voyages on small lakes, rivers and canals where conditions up to and including wind force 4, and significant wave heights up to and including 0.5m may be experienced.

2 General Requirements: recreational craft and their components as referred to in Annex II shall comply with the essential requirements insofar as they apply to them.

2.1 *Hull identification*

Each craft shall be marked with a hull identification number including:
manufacturer's code;
country of manufacture;
unique serial number;

EU regulations will not affect existing boats.

year of production;
model year.
The relevant harmonized standard gives details of these requirements.

2.2 *Builder's plate*
Each craft shall carry a permanently affixed plate mounted separately from the boat identification number containing the following information:
manufacturer's name;
CE marking;
boat design category according to Section 1;
manufacturer's maximum recommended load according to section 3.6;
number of persons recommended by the manufacturer for which the boat was designed to carry when under way.

2.3 *Protection from falling overboard and means of reboarding.*
Depending on the design category, craft shall be designed to minimize the risks of falling overboard and to facilitate reboarding.

2.4 *Visibility from the main steering position*
2.4.1 *For motor boats, the main steering position shall give the operator, while under normal conditions of use (speed and load), good all-round visibility*

2.5 *Owner's manual*
All craft shall be provided with an owner's manual in the official community language or languages which may be determined by the Member State in which it is marketed in accordance with the Treaty. This manual should draw particular attention to the risks of fire and flooding and shall contain the information listed in sections 2.2, 3.6, and 4 as well as the unladen weight of the craft in kilogrammes.

3 Integrity, Structural Requirements:
3.1 *Structure*
The choice and combination of materials and its construction shall ensure the craft is strong enough in all respects. Special attention shall be paid to the boat design category according to section 1, and the manufacturer's

An owner's manual is a good idea, especially for complicated boats.

maximum recommended load according to section 3.6.

3.2 *Stability and freeboard*
The craft shall have sufficient stability and freeboard considering its boat design category according to section 1, and the manufacturer's maximum recommended load according to section 3.6.

3.3 *Buoyancy and flotation*
The craft shall be constructed to ensure that it has buoyancy characteristics appropriate to its design category according to section 1 and the manufacturer's maximum recommended load according to section 3.6. All habitable multihull craft shall be so designed as to have sufficient buoyancy to remain afloat in the inverted position.
Boats of less than 6 metres in length that are susceptible to swamping when used in their design category shall be provided with appropriate means of flotation in the swamped condition.

3.4 *Openings in hull, deck and super-structure*
Openings in hull, deck(s) and superstructure shall not impair the structural integrity of the craft or its weathertight integrity when closed.
Windows, port lights, doors and hatch covers shall withstand the water pressure likely to be encountered in their specific position, as well as pointloads applied by the weight of persons moving on deck.
Through-hull fittings designed to allow water passage into the hull or out of the hull, below the waterline corresponding to the manufacturer's maximum recommended load according to section 3.6, shall be fitted with shut-off means which shall be readily accessible.

3.5 *Flooding*
All craft shall be designed so as to minimize the risk of sinking.
Particular attention should be paid where appropriate to:

Manual bilge pumps are always ready for use.

cockpits and well, which should be self-draining or have other means of keeping water out of the boat interior;
ventilation fittings;
removal of water by suitable pumps or other means.

3.6 Manufacturer's maximum recommended load
The manufacturer's maximum recommended load (fuel, water, provisions, miscellaneous equipment and people (in kilogrammes)) for which the boat was designed as marked on the builder's plate, shall be determined according to the boat design category (section 1), stability and freeboard (section 3.2) and buoyancy and flotation (section 3.3).

3.7 Liferaft stowage
All craft of categories A and B, and craft of categories D and of D longer than 6 metres, shall be provided with one or more stowage points for a liferaft (liferafts) large enough to hold the number of persons the boat was designed to carry as recommended by the manufacturer. This (these) stowage point(s) shall be readily accessible at all times.

3.8 Escape
All habitable multihull craft over 12m long shall be provided with a viable means of escape in the event of inversion.
All habitable craft shall be provided with a viable means of escape in the event of fire.

3.9 Anchoring, mooring and towing
All craft, taking into account their design category and their characteristics, shall be fitted with one or more strong points or other means capable of safely accepting anchoring, mooring or towing loads.

4 Handling Characteristics
The manufacturer shall ensure that the handling characteristics of the craft are satisfactory with the most powerful engine for which the boat is designed and constructed. For all recreational marine engines, the maximum rated engine power shall be declared in the owner's manual in accordance with the harmonized standard.

5 Installation Requirements

5.1 Engines and engine spaces
5.1.1 All inboard mounted engines shall be placed within an enclosure separated from living quarters and installed so as to minimize the risk of fires as well as hazards from toxic fumes, heat, noise or vibration in the living quarters.
Engine parts and accessories that require frequent inspection and/or servicing shall be readily accessible.
5.1.2 Ventilation
The engine compartment shall be ventilated. The dangerous ingress of water into the engine compartment through all intakes must be prevented.
5.1.3 Exposed parts
Unless the engine is protected by a cover or its own enclosure, exposed moving or hot parts of the engine that could cause personal injury shall be effectively shielded.
5.1.4 Outboard engines starting
All boats with outboard engines shall have a device to prevent starting the engine in gear, except:
(a) when the engine produces less than 500N of static thrust;
(b) when the engine has a throttle limiting device to limit the thrust to 500N at the time of starting the engine.

5.2 Fuel systems
5.2.1 General
The filling, storage, venting and fuel supply arrangements and installations shall be designed and installed so as to minimize the risk of fire and explosion.

5.2.2 *Fuel tanks*

Fuel tanks, lines and hoses shall be secured and separated or protected from any source of significant heat. The material the tanks are made of and their method of construction shall be according to their capacity and the type of fuel. All tank spaces shall be ventilated.

Liquid fuel with a flash-point below 55 °C shall be kept in tanks which do not form part of the hull and are:

(a) insulated from the engine compartment and from all source of ignition;

(b) separated from the living quarters.

Liquid fuel with a flash-point equal to, or above 55 °C may be kept in tanks that are integral with the hull.

5.3 *Electrical systems*

Electrical systems shall be designed and installed so as to ensure proper operation of the craft under normal conditions of use and shall be such as to minimize risk of fire and electric shock.

Attention shall be paid to the provision of overload and short-circuit protection of all circuits, except engine starting circuits, supplied from batteries.

Ventilation shall be provided to prevent the accumulation of gases which might be emitted from batteries. Batteries shall be firmly secured and protected from ingress of water.

5.4 *Steering systems*

5.4.1 *General*

Steering systems shall be designed, constructed and installed in order to allow the transmission of steering loads under foreseeable operating conditions.

5.4.2 *Emergency arrangements*

Sailboat and single-engined inboard-powered motor boats with remote-controlled rudder steering systems shall be provided with emergency means of steering the craft at reduced speed.

5.5 *Gas systems*

Gas systems for domestic use shall be of the vapour withdrawal type and shall be designed and installed so as to avoid leaks and the risk of explosion and be capable of being tested for leaks. Materials and components shall be suitable for the specific gas used to withstand the stresses and exposures found in the marine environment.

Each appliance shall be equipped with a flame failure device effective on all burners. Each gas-consuming appliance must be supplied by a separate branch of the distribution system, and each appliance must be controlled by a separate closing device.

Adequate ventilation must be provided to prevent hazards from leaks and products of combustion.

All craft with a permanently installed gas system shall be fitted with an enclosure to contain all gas cylinders. The enclosure shall be separated from the living quarters, accessible only from the outside and ventilated to the outside so that any escaping gas drains overboard. Any permanent gas system shall be tested after installation.

5.6 *Fire protection*

5.6.1 *General*

The type of equipment installed and the layout of the craft shall take account of the risk and spread of fire. Special attention shall be paid to the surroundings of open flame devices, hot areas of engines and auxiliary machines, oil and fuel overflows, uncovered oil and fuel pipes and avoiding electrical wiring above hot areas of machines.

5.6.2 *Fire-fighting equipment*

Craft shall be supplied with fire-fighting equipment appropriate to the fire hazard. Petrol-engine enclosures shall be protected by a fire-extinguishing system that avoids the need to open the enclosure in the event of fire.

Where fitted, portable fire extinguishers shall be readily accessible and one shall be so positioned that it can easily be reached from the main steering position of the craft.

5.7 *Navigation lights*
Where navigation lights are fitted, they shall comply with the 1972 COLREG or CEVNI regulations, as appropriate.

5.8 *Discharge prevention*
Craft shall be constructed so as to prevent the accidental discharge of pollutants (oil, fuel, etc) overboard.
Craft fitted with toilets shall have either:
(a) holding tanks, or
(b) provision to fit holding tanks on a temporary basis in areas of use where the discharge of human waste is restricted.
In addition, any through-the-hull pipes for human waste shall be fitted with valves which are capable of being sealed shut.

Annex II

Components:
1 Ignition-protected equipment for inboard and stern drive engines.
2 Start-in-gear protection devices for outboard engines.
3 Steering wheels, steering mechanisms and cable assemblies.
4 Fuel tanks and hoses.
5 Pre-fabricated hatches and port-lights.

That is the last section of this version of the Boat Safety Scheme. But what does it all mean? It means that new boats built under the EU directive should be a lot safer than some of the things bodged together beforehand. Although some of the terms seem a bit vague and woolly – phrases such as 'Where appropriate' – they are, in fact, anything but. There are over twenty international standards covering the various systems on board, and the boats will have to meet these. Inevitably some boats will not, and the boat builders will be liable for any damage that results. The longer-term result will be more expensive boats, since to abide by and carry out these regulations will cost a lot of money, and boat builders will pass this cost straight on to the public; they have little choice in the matter.

It will be more difficult for the individual building his own boat, but the regulations should be accessible through libraries. Oh dear, this Eurospeak has even got to me, 'accessible' indeed.

— 8 —

Paperwork and Cruising Equipment

Buying a Boat

Sooner or later the boating addiction leads to the purchase of a boat, either your first, or one which is even bigger than the one you have already. Although the plethora of rules and regulations seems to have had the effect of removing the old and tatty, but relatively cheap boats from the market, there is still a lot to be said for buying a low cost and probably somewhat battered wreck as your first boat. The boat club admirals might look down their noses, but those who can get afloat whilst still young can gain enormous experience in such craft, make all those dreadful mistakes and even sink the boat on a bad day, but without risking a huge capital investment. More importantly, all the vital elements of safety and boatmanship can be learned at a time when you are still flexible enough to appreciate it. As the boating enthusiast gets older and hopefully richer, he can graduate to bigger boats, when he will be more confident that a moment's inattention will not send his hugely valuable boat crunching into a lock wall at speed.

The most difficult part of the whole process is deciding what type of boat to buy: there are thousands out there, and no two are exactly the same. First, therefore, you need to identify your own needs. If your desired cruising range is going to include narrow canals, then a boat more than 6ft 10in (2m) wide is not going to be much use. If you have a young family, then a centre cockpit boat with a second bedroom at the stern may well be a good option (earplugs are a good idea, too). If your normal cruising involves fast-flowing rivers or tidal waters, then you will need a boat that can manage about twenty knots if necessary, and that means a large engine.

It is worth spending considerable effort researching just exactly what you do want from a boat before you set out to buy one. This is as true for the tenth boat as it is for the first; everyone's circumstances change, and therefore so also do the needs that the boat has to fulfil. Since there is little point in buying a boat and then finding that it cannot do the job you want it to, a clear idea of your needs is paramount. Once this is understood there is the matter of finding it.

Boat shows and rallies are an excellent place to look at boats and to talk to their owners; in this way it is possible to get a feel for the comfort and handling of the boat that you think might fit the bill. You will discover the drawbacks from talking to the owners, not the sales staff. Don't worry about introducing yourself to a stranger on a boat that you would like to learn about; most boat owners are very friendly, and will be only too keen to discuss the pros and cons of their boat. If they aren't, put it down to experience and just remember the sort of boat it was; you may even find that some marques of boat attract particularly diffident owners!

Once you have decided on the boat type that will suit your needs, it is a matter of finding one you can buy.

Buying a New Boat

New boats are not difficult to find and buy; the sales team will probably be knocking on your door the moment you make an inquiry. They will almost certainly try and persuade you to buy the next size up, the more expensive one, or plaster the one you have chosen with every possible extra (depth sounders are not much use on the canal system); but then, they have a living to earn too. Boats come either as production models, or they are built to order; the production models can usually be delivered quickly, whereas the specially built ones will take longer and will, of course, cost more.

Once you have agreed to purchase a new boat you will need to start on the paperwork. New boats are now going to be covered by the EEC directive on recreational craft, different types of boats being covered by various sections. These standards are only just being introduced, and at present (1994–5) their implementation is sporadic, to say the least. Larger manufacturers have on the whole got the paperwork in order, but some smaller businesses are still learning. New boats will soon have a CE mark on a plate which will also state the builder, the model type and the serial number. There should be a comprehensive user guide and full guarantee for the entire craft. The scheme should become law in this country on 16 December 1995, and be in effect six months later. There will also be many disclaimers regarding liability, and other Eurospeak clauses in this. You should also get a receipt for your money and a bill of sale, which will state the exact details of the boat, who built it, and who bought it, together with all relevant identity, and serial and security numbers. This may seem like a great deal of extra bother, especially to the boat builders, but the previous way of doing business – fork out thousands and pray that nothing goes wrong – was not very satisfactory. Now you can order the boat, pay the cash when you have got it, and *then* pray that nothing goes wrong. The British Marine Industries Federation has a standard contract of sale which most reputable boat builders use.

Boats that are sold with the CE mark have been built by companies that have had their quality control procedures, and to some extent their technical abilities, examined and approved. The CE mark on a new boat automatically means that it complies with the Boat Safety Scheme. Once the boat is four years old it will need a new test certificate, in much the same way as a car.

Where a boat has to be built specially, or heavily customized, it is normal practice for the builder to ask for a reasonable deposit before he carries out the work to create a boat that only *you* want. This shouldn't really be more than 10 per cent; after all, if he doesn't do the customizing you have requested, *you* don't want to lose a large deposit. As before, the BMIF has a standard contract available.

For those who are not confident that they have the expertise to inspect the new boat for faults in adequate detail when it is delivered, it is worth employing a marine surveyor to go over it with a fine toothcomb. Not all boat builders turn out to be perfect examples of their craft, and if there is something wrong with the boat it will need to be identified immediately. It is no good going back to the builder in four years' time when it requires its first Boat Safety Certificate and accusing him of causing the water heater chimney to fail because he inadvisedly shortened it. Even though a boat has a CE mark, this is not a cast-iron guarantee that it will meet every surveyor's interpretation of the standards.

Buying a Secondhand Boat

When it comes to buying secondhand boats, life is more complicated. Once a boat has been about for a while it becomes 'individualized' by its owners, and this process can cover anything from a minor alteration such as changing the curtains, to major structural butchery that leaves the boat dangerous to cruise on a duck pond, never mind a river. In the same way that you choose a new boat, it is worth deciding the type of boat you want before starting to look for a secondhand one. This will save hours of fruitless journeys going to look at boats that are simply unsuited to your needs. Boats are advertised in the classified sections of waterways magazines, boat brokerage businesses and occasionally in local newspapers, but the only real way to tell whether a boat is a great bargain or an expensive heap of junk is to go and see it, and preferably to take it out for a spin on the river.

Those who have a reasonable amount of experience with boats will be able to tell if it has any nasty faults, osmosis or cracks. However, there are plenty of things that can be wrong with a boat, so if you are not confident about everything on board, but still like the look of the vessel, then it is worth arranging for a detailed survey to be done by a professional. This should set your mind at rest that the boat is safe, and good value for the money, and it could warn you of any work that may need to be done. Most boats now have a Safety Certificate (Certificate of Compliance). This scheme was initially introduced in 1990 and so most boats have had to obtain one. If the boat has not got one there may be a good reason – for example, perhaps it was moored on a waterway not administered by British Waterways – but there is a chance that it has a dangerous fault. The certificate is like an MOT for cars, merely stating that the boat was in a correct condition when the surveyor checked it. However, a lot can happen to a boat in three or four years, and not all of it for the best.

There is one golden rule for secondhand boats: the Latin phrase, 'caveat emptor', meaning 'buyer beware'.

Selling a Boat

It is all rather different when it comes to selling your boat. How much is it worth? Are there any faults that you haven't noticed? How will people find out what a bargain it is?

If you are not sure about the value and structural integrity of the boat, then it is best to ask a surveyor to value it and check it over. There is no point in trying to sell a boat that has some dangerous defect; what if a novice bought it, and drowned his family?

The boating press is the best place to advertise the boat: a short and accurate advert will attract the attention of potential buyers; and if you use a photo, make sure that it is a good clear one. The reproduction of these pictures tends to be so small that unless it is of excellent quality the boat will look tiny; the picture needs to have a strong contrast, and the boat must fill at least 80 per cent of the space. And don't forget that when a colour photograph is reproduced as a black-and-white one, only the light levels contrast; so even if there are many different colours, if they are all of the same brightness, the whole picture comes out as a uniform grey.

Once your advert has appeared in the press the phone will start ringing. Half the calls, if not more, will be from other businesses who want to sell it for you. Not all these companies are *bona fide* concerns: there are quite a few who will offer all sorts of wonderful advertising packages, all of which sound like a brilliant bargain, but once they've got your money very little actually happens. Then there are other companies who will phone to say that they already have a client looking for just your type of boat, and that they have been retained by him or her to look for boats. They then offer to introduce this client to you, and quickly mention that there will be a nominal fee for your boat to go on their register. The nominal fee will turn out to be several hundred pounds and the 'client' turns out to be interested only in 1906 motor torpedo boats or such like. Slamming the telephone down is one way of dealing with these people, but the phone gets a bit battered after a while; the most effective policy is to ask them to confirm everything that they have said on the phone in a letter so that you can consider their offer at your leisure. This won't be a problem for a legitimate business, but the sharks will back off at the mention of letters as these can be used as evidence.

If the thought of dealing with all the calls, showing the population over the boat, and generally wasting valuable time does not appeal, it is well worth considering boat brokerage. Many boat yards offer a brokerage service: you simply take the boat to their yard and they advertise it and show potential buyers over it, haggle the price and usually pay the mooring fees. The service costs a percentage of the sale price, but for many people this is well worth the money.

Insurance

Insurance is, surprisingly enough, not compulsory for inland craft as yet, but you would be ill-advised not to have it. The policies available range from basic (minimum) third party cover, up to fully comprehensive cover. Insurers are very specific about their policies and if there is the slightest detail missed out on your disclosure to them, they will use this to avoid paying out on a claim. It is therefore imperative that you inform them of all the relevant details of the boat. There is a huge range of prices for roughly similar policies, and it is worth shopping around. A good example of the kind of difference is that on one occasion a company quoted me £197 for a 30ft (9m) boat, and a broker quoted £86 . . . the broker was selling the company's policy at £111 less than the company, and one assumes still making a profit himself. Insurance is essential, but something of an unknown factor both in the way it is priced and whether the

company will pay out in the event of a claim. Literally as I write (November 1994), the British Waterways General Powers Bill is going through its third reading in the House of Commons, and a clause in this insists that all private craft must have the minimum third party insurance. By the time this book is published the bill will almost certainly have royal assent and insurance will then be mandatory.

Moorings

It is well worth paying a little extra for moorings and getting a spot in a marina or boat club that is secure. Cruisers are vulnerable to theft, and if they are moored out in the back of beyond there is a very good chance that someone will break in. It is not always burglars, either: quite a few homeless vagrants will use a boat as a convenient place to squat on their travels; so if you find that your soap is all gone, the food store ransacked and that any old clothes you left aboard have vanished and been replaced with something that smells as though it has spent a month in a sewage works, then you know why. The other advantage of marinas and boat clubs is their lively social life.

Cruising Equipment

Enough of all this paperwork; after all, half the pleasure of boating is being able to get away from the telephone and the bills at home; who needs reminding about them on the water? Boat hooks are much more interesting.

Boat Hooks and Poles

Boat hooks and poles need a bit of care if they are going to last any length of time. The cheapest in use is the broom stale, very handy

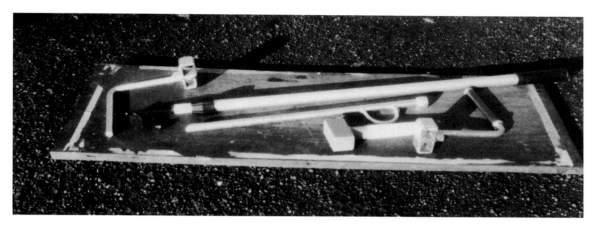

Hooks, poles, spikes and clutter!

and lightweight, but a trifle short; if you want it to last, it is worth treating it with a wood preservative once a year. This is true of any wooden pole or hook. Aluminium poles and hooks are more expensive, but look rather more professional. One-piece poles are very strong along their length, but never use them as a lever or they will crumple up terminally; they don't need any maintenance other than cleaning. Telescopic poles are that much weaker due to their thinner walls; they also need to be kept much cleaner because mud and grit will work its way into the telescopic section and jam up the works. A light coat of oil will keep them moving freely.

Gangplanks

Gangplanks also come in wood and aluminium. Wooden ones are very often bits of scaffold planking found floating in the cut; this is not exactly rated for marine use, however, in fact it is not really supposed to take a person's weight if it is not supported underneath every few feet – the exact distance is determined by its thickness and is stamped on the metal binding on the ends. Most planks need to be seven feet (2m) long, which is well in excess of the usual specification.

The seven foot (2m) length is just handy for propping open awkward lock gates on canals and squeezing the boat through underneath. Still, if you have a wooden gangplank which meets the requirements, treat it liberally with wood preservative, or paint it and keep it as dry as possible. Purpose-made aluminium planks are smart, efficient, and expensive pieces of kit which look absolutely ideal . . . until the non-slip surface on them comes unstuck. This can be replaced if necessary.

Fenders

The humble fender takes a great deal of punishment, crunched between boat and lockside on a regular basis, walloped into gates and thoroughly battered; all of which is exactly what it is designed for. However, it doesn't take long for fenders to start feeling unwanted, and then they seek revenge: if you let them get dirty, they will quickly transfer this mud and grit to the hull, and then grind it in really hard; this will strip the gel coat in a matter of weeks and leave a permanent mark. It is important to keep them clean. Permanently fixed fenders don't suffer from this problem, but they are terribly prone – particularly those on the transom – to coming

New fenders.

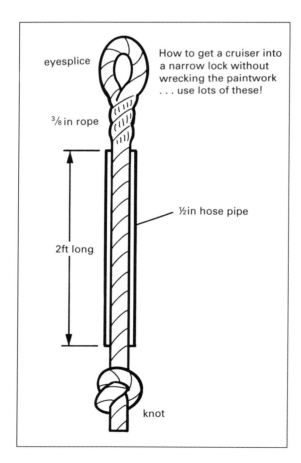

eyesplice

How to get a cruiser into
a narrow lock without
wrecking the paintwork
. . . use lots of these!

⅜ in rope

½in hose pipe

2ft long

knot

Hose pipe fender.

off the boat and taking an entirely different cruise, never to be seen again. Check every few weeks that they are not working loose.

The ordinary plastic inflated fenders age quite rapidly; after a few years they will become hard and brittle as well as scratched to pieces. Once they reach this stage they are not a lot of use on the boat, although they will still be handy on mooring posts and piers.

Tyres are not much use for fenders; they might be alright for narrow boats with their black hulls, but on a nice white hull they will leave grubby black marks that are difficult to remove.

For cruising on narrow canals, fenders are both a blessing and a curse. The narrow locks create an urgent need for plenty of fenders to stop the boat being worn away by all the brickwork, but they also lead to some heart-stopping moments when the fenders wedge between the boat and the lock walls, stopping its movement; when the water keeps going down, but the boat doesn't, a problem has definitely occurred. A simple and inexpensive way to provide some narrow fendering is to thread a yard (metre) of ⅜in (10mm) rope through a piece of ½in (13mm) hosepipe a couple of feet (60cm) long, and dangle plenty of these over the sides. It may look a little odd, but it will keep your nice clean GRP away from that slimy, brick-infested mess. However, none of this will help if you happen to encounter a car under the water, as I did in Birmingham (and plenty of other things besides).

Anchors and Mudweights

The anchor is the last resort when just about everything else has gone wrong, the kind of day when the motor has packed up, the wind and current is whisking the boat towards a weir faster than the speed limit, and it is starting to rain. At this point you will stop muttering that the damn anchor is always in the way and be very glad it is there. The size of the anchor is very dependent on the size of the boat. For boats under 20ft (6m) in length something in the region of 10lb (4.5kg) in weight should be adequate, and between this and 30ft (9m), 20lb (9kg) will be about right. You will need to check what is correct for your boat either with the boat builder or the anchor manufacturer, because it may well be less than this. The anchor will need the same weight of chain attached to it to hold it down on the river bed, and about 36ft (11m) of rope warp from the chain to the anchor point on the boat. The chain and warp will need to be strong enough to withstand the 'snatch' as the anchor bites into the river-bed and pulls the boat up suddenly. One-inch (25mm) link size is usually adequate, though again, the anchor manufacturer will have his own recommended sizes to suit your boat.

It is imperative that you check the condition of the anchor warp every few months. You will look a complete idiot if you have to deploy the anchor, it bites and momentarily saves you from doom, and then the rotten rope snaps and you are back off again towards the weir!

Mudweights are a handy way of keeping the boat stationary in very sheltered waters (canals when there is no wind); all they are is

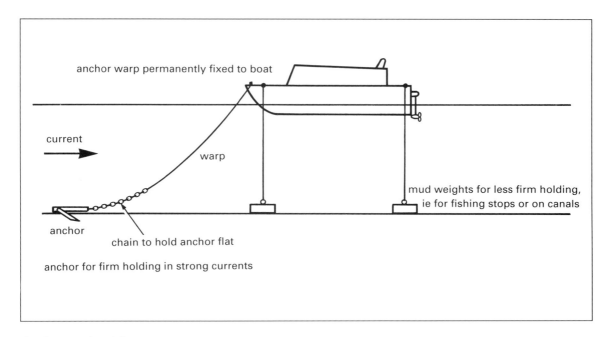

Anchors and weights.

Anchor and mudweight.

a 40lb or 50lb (18 or 23 kg) iron block tied to a warp long enough to allow them to sit on the bottom and tie the boat to. They are excellent for fishing. Breeze blocks do the job just as well, but do not have the same fashionable elegance of a nice old tractor weight or Avery weight.

Ropes

It is very easy to overlook the ropes, and easy enough to trip over them! Every boat needs fore and aft lines, a centre line and several others for specific mooring tasks. There are all manner of makes of rope: sisal, hemp and cotton are the main vegetable-fibre ones, and polypropylene and nylon are the main artificial types, and there is whole art to splicing them and knotting them which I don't propose

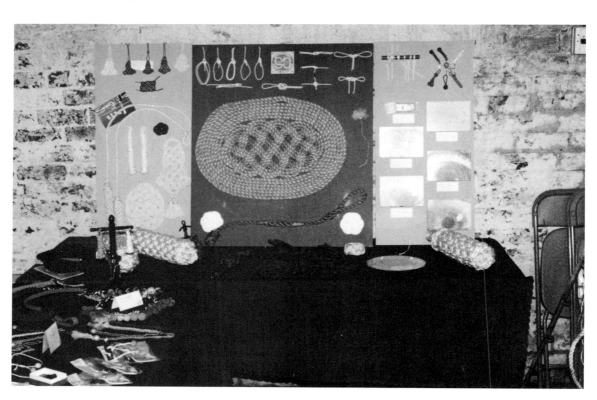

You can do some fancy stuff with rope!

even to contemplate covering here. Rope-work deserves its own book, and there are several very good ones available. Whatever make of ropes you decide to keep on board, do check at least once a month that they are clean, unfrayed, and not going rotten. A damaged rope is likely to break suddenly, and that can be disastrous.

Miscellaneous Hardware

There are other odd bits of hardware that appear on the boat. **Windlasses**, of course; these don't need anything more than a clean to remove that ghastly black grease from the paddle gear. **Mooring spikes** are essential, even though they have a habit of escaping; it is helpful to paint the top end of these with a bright, fluorescent, coloured paint to avoid banging your shins on them. The **lump hammer** for knocking them in will benefit from a coat of strong-coloured paint, too; I shudder to think how many lump hammers I have put down in long grass and never seen again.

The boat will also need a **tool kit**. During a long cruise all sorts of unexpected things can go wrong, and there are times when you simply won't be able to call out the authorized service engineer – if there is one for that particular problem. Gas installations are out of bounds regardless, so if something goes wrong with that system you will just have to live without it. The electrical system has plenty of bits that can blow, light bulbs, fuses and pumps. Your tool kit will need enough tools to get at these parts, and the spares box will need the correct spares in it, basically a duplicate of every bulb and fuse on the boat. Always remember that when a fuse blows it almost always does it because something else has drawn too much power; something like a short-circuit. Never replace the fuse with one of a higher rating, and always look to see what caused it to blow. The engine is likely to need its own set of basic spares, fan belts, spark plugs and ignition components. Every engine

is different, so it isn't possible to draw up a list that would make sense, but you will probably find a basic list of suggested spares in the owner's manual.

Silicon sealant is always handy to have around a boat. It can be used to stop new leaks around windows, it can even be used to make an emergency seal around a hole in the hull if you have just run over a car. **String** and **sticky tape** always have a place in a tool kit. A pair of **wire cutters** and a very sharp **knife** are useful for clearing rubbish off the propeller. As a boat gets older, things like **spare control cables** can be helpful if you don't know how well maintained they were before you took them on. An **electric torch**, preferably one that can be stood and pointed in a specific direction, is a good idea.

A small **first-aid kit** is worth keeping beside the tool kit: there are plenty of sharp corners on boats and locks for a good supply

Why not do a first-aid course; you never know when you might need it.

of plasters to be essential, and a few larger bandages are helpful. A bottle of painkillers can be included; if you have small children, pre-packed doses of oral rehydration salts are extremely valuable. Unless you are a qualified first-aider, much more than this is irrelevant; so why not do a first-aid course?

The **life-rings** on the boat must be kept clean and ready for use. There are now throwable buoyant life-lines which require far less storage space, are much less effort to throw any distance, and don't knock the victim unconscious if they hit his head. These have to be in addition to the life-rings to meet the Safety Scheme, but they are well worth getting on board.

It is worth checking who on board is a swimmer. It is quite easy to slip off a cruiser, and rivers are not like swimming pools: if you fall in you are quickly disorientated, cold and of course wet. Even a strong swimmer can be in trouble in these circumstances, and non-swimmers and children are best fitted with buoyancy aids whenever they are on board. For all of the gentle humour of the waterways, this is no joke: it is an essential practice that really must be adhered to.

Safety

Perhaps choosing the last few paragraphs of the book to emphasize the dangers of the water is a bit tactless; after all, there are very, very few accidents on the inland waterways. Nevertheless, the safety and security of the crew are the most important consideration of all, which is why it is so important to look after the boat well, and to care for all its structure and systems: thus you can be sure that whenever you want it, it is there ready and waiting.

The inland waterways are a fascinating mixture of natural and man-made environments. There are wild, wide open spaces, full of sky and a silence broken only by the call of birds; there are busy junctions and factories humming with industry, brick-lined caverns where a dark canal winds through a pall of smog only to emerge into a sunlit cutting ablaze with spring flowers in the heart of a city. There is just so much to see, and a well looked after boat is the companion who will take you there.

The end.

Index